When Y

Also by the same author:

Heal The Sick (Hodder & Stoughton)

When You Pray

Personal encounters with God

REGINALD EAST

Marshall Pickering

Marshall Morgan and Scott
Marshall Pickering
3 Beggarwood Lane, Basingstoke, Hants RG23 7LP, UK

First published in 1986 by
Marshall Morgan and Scott Publications Ltd
Part of the Marshall Pickering Holdings Group
A subsidiary of the Zondervan Corporation

British Library CIP Data

East, Reginald
When you pray: personal encounters with God
1. Prayer
I. Title
248.3′2 BV210.2

ISBN 0 551 01338 9

Text set in Plantin by
Brian Robinson Ltd, North Marston, Bucks.
Printed in Great Britain by Hazell Watson & Viney,
Member of the BPCC Group, Aylesbury, Bucks.

Contents

Preface

This book is written for the person in the pew. An increasing number are dissatisfied with the prayer they have been taught and are searching for a prayer relationship with God which will satisfy them spiritually and emotionally. This is a heartening sign. The same need is seen among people outside the Church who are turning in such directions as to Transcendental Meditation for the expression and satisfaction of their inner need as they react against the materialistic society in which we live. As Christians we believe that Christ alone can give us the satisfaction we long for.

The Holy Spirit is among us, evoking this desire for God. Much is happening through the charismatic renewal to give new vision in prayer and worship. He is also enlivening and unfolding our present forms of worship as well as bringing to us the treasures of past writings by people who have hungered for and found God.

This book is an attempt to show something of the way forward for those today to whom God is giving this same desire for Himself and who know instinctively that they must find it through prayer and worship. It is hoped it may be a signpost on the road. Some of the material has already been given as teaching and requests have been received to put it into writing. This gives some confidence that what is written may be of help to others also.

Reginald East

1

The God to whom we pray

The capacity for being in conscious relationship with God in prayer belongs only to human beings. This above all differentiates us from the rest of creation. Such an ability is our loftiest privilege and joy. To what greater height could we ascend than to live in a personal relationship with the God from whom all things have come? What else could offer greater potential and adventure to us? In a world where adventure has been denied to so many, everyone has the opportunity to live a life of adventure into God Himself. This is an eternal adventure as well as being the highest and most satisfying of all.

All human beings have an innate ability to pray but, quite apart from the numerous influences and experiences which nullify this ability in the lives of countless people, whether and how we pray depends upon the sort of God in which we believe. If, as with many of the religions of the past, we believe that God is someone to be feared, we will do our best to keep on the right side of Him and propitiate Him. In other words, we will protect ourselves from Him as far as we can. There are many people today who see God primarily as judge and this inevitably conditions the way they pray. All of us, until we meet and know the true God as revealed to us in Jesus Christ, form our conception of God at least partly from our experience of authority. We make God in the image of our parents or some other authority figure.

So, first, as we look at this activity of prayer, we should note what the Christian faith tells us of God. The full appreciation of Him will be through a long road of learning and change, and will never be complete this side of heaven, but to be clear in our minds about the basic revelation of God cannot but help us along the way. We will give attention to the primary revelation of God in Christ—that He is love and that He is holy.

God is love

In the Christian faith the central revelation is that 'God is love' (1 John 4.16), and John goes on to say 'and he who abides in love abides in God, and God abides in him'. With such a God, far from protecting ourselves from Him, we are drawn by love to abide (or live) 'in' Him because He lives 'in' us. The God revealed by Jesus Christ is one who came 'to seek and to save the lost', (Luke 19.10) and so to draw us into a relationship of love with Himself.

But what do we mean when we say 'God is love'? It does not merely mean that He is a loving person. That could suggest that He is kindly disposed towards us, but with the likelihood that sometimes He might not be so loving in His attitude. No, when we say 'God is love' we mean that He is love itself. That is to say, nothing can stop Him loving us. He has no alternative but to love us because He is love itself. So no matter what we do to Him, whether we love Him, hate Him, spit on Him, drive nails into His hands and feet, it cannot alter His love for us. We may grieve His heart, but He will still love us. So, when they did some of these things to our Lord Jesus Christ, His only reaction was to say, 'Father, forgive them'. He absorbed into Himself all the evil that came to Him and transmuted it into love.

Because He *is* love, our Lord had no alternative but to come to save us. Perfect love could never have left mankind in the fearful state in which it was and is. Christ had to come. In the same way He comes to each one of us now. We may not receive Him, but He is still seeking every human being. He shares what is happening to every human life, for He said, 'As you did it to one of the least of these my brethren, you did it to me' (Matt. 25.40). This means that Christ is totally involved in everything that happens in every human life as if it were His own life.

It follows that Christ wants to have a full part in the life of each one of us, to share the bad as well as the good. He does not wait until we get a bit better before He loves us and wants to share our lives. He loves us now. He has loved us from the foundation of the world and will love us into eternity.

And so, just as Jesus came into the world at His incarnation at Bethlehem, so He comes to each one of us now. He may have to stand outside many of us, but His desire is to enter into us and live there. He said,

'If a man loves me, he will keep my word, and my Father will love him, and we will come to him and make our home with him' (John 14.23). If God makes His home in us, then we can be in personal relationship with Him. The way to an intimate prayer life with Him is then open to us.

To speak of God as love, however, inevitably raises the formidable question of suffering. The world is full of suffering, much of it coming to undeserving people as, for example, refugees torn from their homes and those suffering from drought and earthquake. Much ink has been spilled over this heart-rending question and, apart from the suffering caused by human sin, there is no satisfactory answer. This is not the place for a full enquiry. What can be attempted is to make some remarks which will help us in our desire to enter into prayer.

We need first to accept the fact that with this world as it is, suffering of some kind is inevitable. Sin always brings suffering with it, and we all feel its effects. For this reason the New Testament makes it quite clear that the life of a Christian will not be an easy one. Jesus warned us that 'The gate is narrow and the way is hard, that leads to life' (Matt. 7.14). The natural attitude of most of us is to seek for protection, but in that way we lose so much of the adventure of our life in Christ. As He Himself graphically expressed it: 'For whoever would save his life will lose it; and whoever loses his life for my sake and the gospel's will save it' (Mark 8.35). This is one of the great paradoxes of life.

It is at this point of suffering that we are most

clearly shown God's love. For God's reaction to it is the cross. The cross is at the centre of our faith and our faith is centred on the overcoming of sin and the suffering which it breeds. In the cross God shows us that He is responsible for the situation since He is Creator and there at the cross He is receiving in Himself the effect of His creation and is also dealing with it. So Christ entered the arena of sin and within it showed and offered His power over it. In fact He showed that suffering is the only way to break sin's power and influence, provided that it is the action of love.

Hence the New Testament teaches us a very positive approach towards suffering. We are encouraged to love, bless, forgive and pray for those who cause it. If such a way of disciplining us seems hard, we are to realise that God is treating us as sons in order that we may share His life fully. For if we are to have the full dignity of being His children, we must share fully His own life and ministry, and that includes suffering. Paul puts this clearly before us in Romans 8.14–17. We should note particularly verse 17: 'If children, then heirs, heirs of God and fellow heirs with Christ, *provided we suffer with him* in order that we may also be glorified with him' (italics mine). In this, Paul is one with John, who makes it clear in his Gospel that the glory of Christ was His death on the cross; see for example, 'Father the hour has come; glorify thy Son that the Son may glorify thee' (John 17.1). So as we try to follow the way of Christ, we are making the most positive contribution possible in the struggle against suffering.

We may go so far as to say that for the majority of us there is need of suffering in some form in order to keep us close to God, at least in the earlier part of our pilgrimage. When life is easy we tend to become slack and so often it is at times of trouble, sorrow and heartbreak that we are driven back to Him. As we well know, many are brought to Christ through tragedy.

So we have to make a choice. Suffering can either have a negative effect upon us or it can bring out the best in us. In prayer the Holy Spirit can lead us to the right choice and make it possible for us to accept suffering. Love, then, does not mean sentimentality nor being coddled. It has realism. It means willing the best for anyone. It means accepting and doing whatever will bring God into the situation. And God, in His love for us, will use whatever He knows to be necessary to help us to live in union with Him and share in His way of working.

Learning under God to accept suffering in this way makes us more mature and so God can use us. We are taken into the deeper things of God and of our own personality, and what we learn will benefit others. This is what Paul teaches us in 2 Corinthians when he writes, God 'helps us in all our troubles, so that we are able to help others who have all kinds of troubles, using the same help that we ourselves have received from God' (1.4, GNB). Those words were written out of hard experience.

Suffering, then, hard and bewildering as it may be to us at times, is neither a refutation of, nor a bar to, the love of God. In our lives with Him, even during the difficult times, He is with us in tenderness and encouragement. It is His presence, sharing it all, which makes all the difference, and it is prayer which makes possible the awareness and experience of His presence. Because of prayer we prove the reality of the words of 1 Peter 1.8, 'Without having seen him you love him', and by it we learn, like Noah, to 'walk with God'.

God is holy

The thought of God's holiness may not be so acceptable to us because of some presentations of Jehovah in the Old Testament. He is at times portrayed in terrifying terms and so the 'awe-fulness' of God can have frightening associations. If these came early in life they may still linger strongly within a person even if, as an adult, we see God much more in terms of Jesus Christ.

Another aspect of God's holiness in the Old Testament is that of separateness. In Moses' time, for example, only Moses himself was permitted to approach Jehovah on the holy mountain. Later, in the holy of holies in the temple, God was not to be approached by His people. Only the high priest had this privilege.

So, because of the associations, the idea of the holiness of God may not be a welcoming one for some people. To this we may add the connotation of pharisaical sanctimoniousness, which also can make it off-putting to us.

Jesus, however, provides a totally different picture. In one sense He is separate from us in that He is sinless and we are not. But His very sinlessness broke the power of human sin and cosmic evil, the very things which separate us from Him. His holiness is therefore not only the means of our salvation but also the assurance that truth and right will ultimately prevail in the universe. Otherwise the future could be a terror, and life meaningless.

It is true also that our Lord's sinlessness can appear disturbing to those who do not wish to face their own sin, or cannot resist indulgence. Even so, we find that we are held gently in the divine mercy which in the end leads us to better things.

Our Lord's very coming demonstrates His longing to be one with us and the Gospels show how totally He identified Himself with the underprivileged. The 'sinners' of His day—the down and outs, the ones who lived as Gentiles, the prostitutes, the ordinary Jews—flocked to Him. His holiness was warm and attractive and drew them to Him.

When we speak of our Lord's holiness and the absence in Him of sin, we are saying, in effect, that there were no barriers in Him to the flow of the love of God. God's love poured out of Him because there were no blockages of forbidding emotions of criticism, ridicule, jealousy or contempt. There were no mixed motives, nothing to cause distrust or fear. In His compassion He identified with the people and their needs. He was one with them, He felt for them and they knew it. So they flocked to Him.

The incident of the prostitute in Simon's house which Luke records for us is a classic example. This woman came *because* Jesus was holy. What He was drew her to Him and made her weep at His feet for what she was. His holiness, which was so attractive, convicted her and made her long to be like Him. She must have known in her heart that forgiveness and acceptance were awaiting her. Had she not, one cannot imagine her facing the condemnation and contempt of Simon and his guests. So it is with us all. It is not by being told we are sinners that we are brought to repentance. It is by seeing the beauty of a holy life which convicts us and makes us long to be the same. No one can so convict as Jesus does.

So, like the common people of Jesus' day, we can with freedom and naturalness come to God. Paul calls this 'boldness'. Happily this can never mean an easy familiarity. The prostitute did not come to our Lord with familiarity. She saw the majestic stature of Christ but she knew that the majesty longed to meet her need and, more, wanted her herself. So her response was uninhibited, even compulsive, but represented humility and total longing. Because of what she saw in Jesus, she was determined to be changed. Who could do this but He? So she was drawn.

When we glimpse the true holiness of God as Christ Jesus demonstrates it, far from being repelled, we are drawn to Him. Truly, and thankfully, we are convicted of our condition and cannot have peace until something is done about it, but this is because we want Him. His words can haunt us, 'Blessed are the pure in heart, for they shall see God' (Matt. 5.8). It is our longing to 'see' God that makes us pray, 'Create in me a clean heart, O God' (Ps. 51.10). We pray like this because we want to live close to Jesus.

Naturally, the life of holiness is one of growth, and

some of us have grown more than others. We all have problems. Perhaps for some it is of having little awareness of sin. If our prayer develops, God will deal with that. With others it may be that they have not moved from confession of sin to the receiving of God's forgiveness. Perhaps a wrong conception of God or their inability to forgive themselves may be at the root. Others may be disheartened because of the persistence of besetting sins. In this situation we need to realise that such sins derive from our two basic instincts to survive and to reproduce. All our self-assertive and sexual sins come from these two instincts and God will not remove the instincts. They will be with us all our lives and we will not rise to perfection in this life.

So we should not lose heart over our sins. What is important is that we take Jesus into our instincts so that they come under His control and are slowly moulded to operate as their Creator intended. We can do the same with the particular sins which emanate from the instincts. By taking our Lord *into* them we give Him the opportunity to deal with them from the inside. If we keep Him out, they remain unchanged. This applies to all our sins, including the ones of which we are most ashamed, such as our vicious reactions to hurts and our sexual aberrations. The Incarnation means that God wants to be in where our sins are to remove and cleanse us of them. Christ's holiness, then, far from separating Him from us, impels Him to share a battle with us against our sin.

Neither the thought of God's holiness nor the shame of our sin should therefore keep us from God, and that means from prayer. In the enfolding love of God we are forgiven sinners and we can trust the Holy Spirit both to pour the love of God into our hearts and to give us the longing to be holy. So we can rejoice to be, as Paul encourages us to be, the temple of God. What better provision could God make for us to be one with Him in prayer?

2

Our approach to God

What has been said so far indicates that we can have a personal relationship with God. If prayer is the expression of such a relationship, then it must be a meeting with Him. It is quite possible to pray to God and not meet Him. When you ask people how they would describe prayer, they give answers such as 'talking to God', 'thanking God', 'asking for help', 'praying for needs', 'praying for His will to be done'. These things are certainly part of our prayer life, but they can all happen without there being any real personal contact with God. Sometimes the definition is given: 'Prayer is conversation with God: it is two-way.' This is a much better description, but when the further question is asked, 'And what do you hear of God's part in the conversation?' the answer may not be too clear. This is not at all surprising because to hear God clearly is not easy. What one senses, however, is that such a description may be made lightly without representing an encounter with God.

The heart of prayer is desire for God. We pray because we want to be with God Himself, even though within that desire we make requests for our needs. The opening words of Psalm 63 communicate this clearly, 'O God, you are my God, and I long for you. My whole being desires you; like a dry, worn-out, and waterless land, my soul is thirsty for you' (GNB). Such an intense desire for God may not yet have arisen in our hearts, but it is this longing which the Holy Spirit wants to evoke in us and which grows as our prayer develops.

Meeting God is an act of personal relationship, but it is not exactly the same as two human beings relating to each other. God has given us personality but although we speak of Him as a person, He is, as C. S. Lewis put it, 'beyond personality'. God, Jesus taught us, is Spirit and we worship Him in spirit. It is Spirit to spirit. In the early stages of prayer such a relationship may be difficult to comprehend, but as we progress in our encounter with God in prayer, the Holy Spirit will lead us to become more at home in such a meeting. We may not feel His presence because feeling is the effect of emotion and spirit is not emotion. But we can become aware of Him and at times God may make this awareness a strong experience. If we try to grasp this idea and set out to remain 'in the Spirit', He will lead us on a search for God which will never cease even though our response may vary and the road now and again be hard, even though at times we may seem to be getting nowhere. But no prayer offered to God genuinely is lost or unused by Him. He can transmute even selfish prayer for, when we pray, we give Him something to use.

The central aim in prayer, then, should be to set out to get into personal touch with God and spend time with

Him. Our Lord has told us that the eternal life which we have in Him is this personal relationship: 'This is eternal life, that they know thee the only true God, and Jesus Christ whom thou hast sent' (John 17.3). So to spend time in fellowship with God is living eternal life. This fellowship comes only by making our prayer a personal meeting with Him. Furthermore, the highest end of eternal life is to worship and adore God. This is the main activity of the angels and will be ours in the next world. As we learn to meet God in prayer we are in due course led to adore Him. This becomes inevitable as soon as we discern something of God's presence. And true adoration is the most selfless activity of the human personality.

Further, to adore leads us to put God in His rightful place, which is at the centre of our lives. As such He is given freedom to act in and through each of us within the vast spectrum of His ministry to the world. Putting meeting with God, therefore, as the object of prayer does not mean that service for God and for humanity is unimportant. Rather, in the ocean of human need, God can guide us to the small amount of service each of us has to give. Not only does God alone know all human need but He also knows how best to use our prayer to meet it. That being the case, we can offer our prayer to Him and leave Him to decide where to apply the spiritual power thus released. We can be pretty sure that, in some way, we shall be involved with our prayer.

Being oneself with God

As the love and the holiness of God together draw us to Him, and since He has gone to such lengths in Christ to bring us to Himself, it means we can be fully ourselves with Him. He wants us. We do not, for example, have to put on our 'prayer face'. God knows exactly what we are like. He is aware of every thought in our heads, and so we might as well be natural with Him. Note Hebrews 4.13, '. . . before him no creature is hidden, but all are open and laid bare to the eyes of him with whom we have to do.' Because of this, God is the one and only person with whom we can be totally ourselves. It is a useless activity trying to hide anything or trying to appear to be what we are not, so we might as well be just ourselves. As such we are wanted, loved and welcomed by God and so we are able to rest in Him. What a relief it is to be totally oneself and resting in God. As Corrie Ten Boom used to say, 'Don't wrestle, nestle.' So we are in the extraordinary situation that it is with the only perfect sinless One that sinners can be free, natural and at peace.

This comforting discovery was made long ago. Moses, for example, when he was having a bad time in the desert said to the Lord, 'Why have you treated me so badly? Why are you displeased with me? Why have you given me the responsibility of all these people? I didn't create them or bring them to birth! Why should you ask me to act like a nurse and carry them in my arms like babies all the way to the land you promised to our ancestors? Where could I get enough meat for all these people? They keep whining and asking for meat. I can't be responsible for all these people by myself; it's too much for me! If you are going to treat me like this, take pity on me and kill me, so that I won't have to endure your cruelty any longer' (Num. 11.1–15, GNB). How many people have felt something like that at times? With the same frankness, Elijah tells the Lord that he has had enough of it and wants only to die (1 Kgs. 19.4). In the Acts of the Apostles that fine Christian, Ananias, when told to go to Saul, patiently informed the Lord of what sort of person Saul was and why he had come to Damascus (9.13)! Even our dear Lord Himself, in Gethsemane, could ask His Father, 'All things are possible for you. Take this cup of suffering away from me' (GNB), before He came to the irrevocable decision of the cross. We may add the many examples of such naturalness in the Psalms, such as Psalm 77.3–10.

Our Lord's example and the example of the great servants of God encourage us to be ourselves with God. If we are feeling disheartened, for example, we can say to Him, 'Lord, I feel so disheartened today that I just want to give up, but I come to you just the same.' Or, if we are angry with someone and cannot yet forgive, as we pray we can say to God, 'Lord, you know how badly I feel about . . . . . My heart is full of hurt and I want to hurt back. Help me through this as I pray.' Or, 'Lord, I don't feel like praying, so lead me to want you.' These are *good* prayers because they are honest and show that beneath all the surface disturbance there is an underlying desire for God. But to go to prayer feeling like that while behaving towards God as though everything in the garden is lovely, is *bad* prayer because it is false. The way to God is hindered by such an attitude.

Prayer, then should be a true meeting between God,

who is perfectly real, and ourselves who are trying to be real also. In such a relationship we can know that we are fully accepted by God. Such an acceptance does not mean, of course, that God is content to leave us as we are nor to condone what is wrong. His longing is to bring us to perfection, but since we can be at one with Him without fear or condemnation, the way is open on both sides for the process of cleansing, change and growth to take place.

God within

A prayer relationship of such closeness and intimacy is possible primarily because, as we have already mentioned, God gives Himself to us. It seems that many people think of God as outside them, even in the sky. He is, of course. He is everywhere. But this expresses a distant relationship with Him, and, if prayer is not going too well, no relationship at all. Scripture teaches us otherwise. The great mystery 'hidden for ages and generations but now made manifest to his saints', Paul tells us, is 'Christ in you, the hope of glory' (Col. 1.26, 27). So God's best gift to us is of Himself. In the parable of the labourers in the vineyard, all were given the same wage. If we put this on a spiritual level, then the 'wages' are God Himself. We can all receive the same 'wage'—God Himself.

Therefore, if we want God, we can receive Him into the centre of our being. Prayer then means that we turn our attention and affection towards the God who is within us. This clearly demands that we invite Him to come within us and that we be willing to put ourselves into His hands. Unless we welcome such a situation, our prayer relationship will not develop. This inner presence of God means that nothing in our lives need be out of His care. Whatever happens, He shares it, is involved and will work with us in it. We can have a similar relationship to the relationship Jesus had with His Father: 'I am not alone, for the Father is with me' (John 16.32).

Perhaps it ought to be said that, when we are in this awareness of God's presence, it can be uncomfortable at times. None of us is perfect and therefore the temptation and desire for sin will occur. We may long to give way to anger, resentment, jealousy, self-indulgence and lust, or they may be a natural reaction to what happens to us. At these times we may want our Lord to be as far away as possible but spiritual growth comes as we let the temptation or sin drive us on to God for help. He is well aware that 'the spirit indeed is willing, but the flesh is weak' (Mark 14.38). We are driven to God when our love for Him is greater than our desire to sin, but this is where most of us often fall down. However, as we co-operate with our Lord, we improve because of His ready help.

Fortunately God knows us inside out, and has promised never to fail us nor forsake us (Heb. 13.5) whatever our spiritual or moral condition. So, with Paul, we should not lose heart but constantly endeavour to put ourselves into the hands of God, believing that He will lead us unerringly along this path of prayer. Within us He is able to make those radical changes in our nature which are necessary for the growing richness of our prayer union with Him.

3

Getting down to it

It might be helpful at this point to refer to some practical matters which have an effect upon our prayer. Each one of us is a unique person and the way we pray will be characteristic of our own nature. Nevertheless, there are considerations which can assist us all. One is the position of the body. We should adopt the position which most makes it possible to forget the body so that our full attention may be on God. That means we should find out whether it normally helps to kneel, sit or lie down. God is not dishonoured when we pray sitting or lying down. What dishonours Him is slack and inattentive prayer.

We are also creatures of habit, and forming habits conducive to prayer facilitates the entry into and the practice of it. We should fix a daily time and place. The time should be when we are fresh and so able to give our best attention to our Lord, as well as when we know we are least likely to be disturbed. For many of us this time is the early morning, but some may choose, for example, the early evening before the evening activities take place. To keep to the same time helps us to get down to prayer straight away. Those who work in a big city may decide to pray in a church near to their work during part of their lunch break.

Whatever time and place we choose, we should in any case start the day with God. One help with this is to go to sleep in a state of prayer. We shall then wake with God. So we can offer ourselves and the day to Him.

It is a positive help, in forming our regular habits of prayer, to pray always in the same place and position. Some people find that the placing of religious symbols in a selected part of a room adds to the sense of its being a place apart.

The length of time we spend in prayer is also important. This should be fixed sensibly, perhaps a little longer than we think we can manage. Not to fix such a period can lead to the length of time diminishing: difficulty, human weakness or circumstances can cause the length of time to be whittled away almost without our realising it (and they will certainly weaken our effort in prayer). So we need to hold to this period even if the prayer is disappointing, for it is essential to train ourselves. As we progress in prayer, the length of time can increase. It will be desire for God which will most govern that increase.

Alone with God

Such careful attention to our prayer follows the teaching of our Lord in the Sermon on the Mount. There our Lord says, 'When you pray, go into your room and shut the door and pray to your Father who is in secret' (Matt. 6.6). There is a note of determination in those words. We are to get away from the normal run of life's activities—the book, record player, radio, television, study, recreation, etc.—go to a place apart, and shut the door on all else but God. There we are with our heavenly Father in secret session. This is the most intimate relationship of our life where all is excluded but God and ourself. What passes between the two is known to no one else.

This teaching demonstrates the importance of our personal prayer in Jesus' eyes. For Him, everything had its source in His prayer-relationship with His Father. So His teaching is a reflection of His own prayer life. He must have had His own 'secret place' (JB and NEB). In the 'secret place' with God alone, He can exert His influence and action in the centre of our being. This is the 'reward' we receive (v. 6b). It is, in fact, the gift of God Himself.

For this to happen, we need to leave the action to God. That is to say, we must not fill the time with a wordy concentration on our own seeming needs. We are there to be as attentive and sensitive to God as we can and so to be open to His movement within us. Because of this, our Lord continues in His teaching, 'And in praying do not heap up empty phrases as the Gentiles do; for they think that they will be heard for their many words. Do not be like them, for your Father knows what you need before you ask him' (6.7–8).

It seems difficult for many of us to believe what Jesus says and so we use our prayer times to pester

God and even try to twist His arm in an attempt to get from Him the things we think we need or to save us from what we fear. But our Lord has it the other way round. In His earthly life, it was what His Father wanted and did that mattered to Him. He said, 'I always do what is pleasing to him' (John 8.29) and He told us that the words He spoke He received from His Father and that the Father did the mighty works through Him (John 14.10). So our Lord's own prayer took the form of the teaching He has given us. That is, He listened and opened Himself to His Father. He therefore wants us to learn to pray in the same way; to turn our thoughts and fears from ourselves on to God and to open ourselves to Him for His work in us.

Our Lord says that we can do this because our Father is well aware of our needs before we ask Him and is quite capable of meeting them. Perhaps our very insistence on them may hinder His provision, while, on the other hand, the putting of God at the centre of our prayer and affection may give Him the very means of meeting our needs.

In the next chapter a method of prayer is outlined which, it is hoped, will help the reader to enter into a way of prayer which more closely follows the teaching of our Lord in the Sermon on the Mount. This is prayer of a more contemplative nature. In the past there has been an assumption by many that contemplative prayer is only for the very few who ascend into the loftier realms of prayer, while those of us of the rank and file spiritually should be content with intercession or meditation on the Bible (which, incidentally, is principally activity of the mind, not prayer, though it feeds the soul and can lead into prayer).

We are *all* made to share the life of God, to love and adore Him and to gaze upon Him. This applies to this world as well as the next. For all Christians, as Paul would say, 'there is no distinction'. Shepherds as well as sages adored at the manger. So we may all awaken to the expectation that a contemplative form of prayer which most satisfies our longing for God is possible. Some may take to it more readily than others, but none need be excluded.

Perseverance in prayer

Prayer is not easy. Although it is part of our God-given nature it does not come naturally, apart from the cry of help when things are bad. It is as well to accept this state of affairs, for then it will help us not to give up too easily. Prayer entails determination and perseverance. Our Lord gave us two parables about prayer and both are calls to persevere. One is of a man knocking up his neighbour in the middle of the night for some bread (Luke 11.5 ff). As Luke gives it, this parable is part of the teaching that Jesus gives in response to the disciples' request, 'Lord, teach us to pray.' In His reply Jesus gave the Lord's Prayer, following it immediately with this story to point out that prayer demands persistence. He continued, 'And I tell you, Ask, and it will be given you; seek, and you will find; knock, and it will be opened to you', all of which give the impression of determination and persistence. The other parable is that of the widow and the judge (Luke 18.1 ff), and we are told, 'Jesus told his disciples a parable to teach them that they should always pray and never become discouraged' (GNB).

So we should clearly understand that prayer, like love, has a large element of will in it. We should realise that this does not make it any less acceptable to God. The simple fact is that unless we take it seriously enough to work at it, we will not get very far and prayer will continue to be a disappointment. If we are beginning or making a new beginning to our prayer adventure, it can help to arrange with another person to have your prayer time simultaneously. The desire not to let the other down is an incentive to be faithful.

It will encourage us to remember that God is continually present with us and will never go away. He has made us to be in a prayer-relationship with Himself and so He is ready and waiting for us to pray. The Lady Julian of Norwich expressed this attractively when she wrote, 'Our Lord is greatly cheered by our prayer. He looks for it and he wants it.' She also had words from our Lord which are an encouragement to us all, especially in the difficult periods:

> Pray inwardly, even if you do not enjoy it. It does good, even though you feel nothing, see nothing. Yes, even though you think you are doing nothing. For when you are dry, empty, sick, or weak, at such a time is your prayer most pleasing to me though you find little enough to enjoy in it.

One cannot over-emphasise the need to persevere in and to make a strong habit in prayer, especially in the early stages. Until that is forged we will not enter into the centre of prayer because we will still be grappling with peripheral matters. To continue like that is, in itself, a disheartening process and will very likely end in our giving up prayer altogether. 'Keep on going on' is an excellent maxim.

4

A method of prayer to meet with God

A method of prayer is now offered by means which large numbers of people have been able to make their time of prayer a satisfying meeting with God. It is a method which observes our Lord's teaching of prayer being a personal encounter with God without much speaking on our part (see Chapter 3). It therefore puts prayer the right way round in that the initiative is left to God. Our part is so to be with Him that we may open ourselves to Him in order that He may be free to move in His love and wisdom.

In this, two things are needed. One is to come to quietness of body and mind and the other is to enter the welcoming world of silence. As these two combine, we can become sensitive and attentive to God. To arrive at such tranquillity takes time, so it cannot be a hurried business. However, as we continue we improve and in time we fall naturally into a state of tranquillity when we turn to prayer.

When most of us begin to try to be tranquil, we are

surprised at the amount of tension we have, both of body and mind. So our first need is to learn to relax. If this proves difficult with any part of the body, then those muscles should first be tensed and then relaxed until tension goes. For example, the facial muscles can be screwed up and then relaxed; the neck can be stretched and then brought to rest; hands clenched and relaxed, and so with any muscles which need this treatment.

Entering into inner silence entails the quietening of our thoughts and emotions so that we may concentrate our attention upon God. This, combined with relaxation of the body, comes with practice but the suggestions which follow have been found helpful. You will probably require special help to get to the root cause of deeply disturbed emotions. The subject of silence is given more attention in the next chapter.

We will now move through the five stages which can bring us to meet our Lord face to face in inner silence and there to commune with Him. If this seems a complicated procedure, we can be assured that with a little practice the stages will merge into one. They will become part of ourselves and take place naturally, so that we are quickly in communion with God.

Stage 1. A comfortable position

Sit right back in the chair, back straight and head up. Have legs uncrossed to obviate numbness and pins and needles. Ankles may be crossed since this does not have that effect. Close the eyes. Now take a few slow, gentle but deep breaths. Push the diaphragm down as the air enters the lungs, so that the whole of the lungs are filled. This and the following stages can also be done in a lying down position.

Stage 2. Relaxing the body

Now let the body come to rest. Relax the muscles of the face and work down the body, neck, shoulders, arms, hands, trunk, legs, feet. Allow the chair to take the total support so that the muscles are released from any action and the whole body comes to a state of rest. Give yourself time to enjoy the luxury of feeling your body so at rest that you have no desire to move even a finger.

Stage 3. Quietening the mind

Now the mind has to come to rest. Deliberately put aside problems, anxieties and work. The movement now is to get the mind still so that it may concentrate on God. Pictures which speak to you of peace and rest may help. Use whatever comes naturally—a picture of Jesus, a scene from the Bible or a devotional symbol. Some may find a lovely scene of nature more helpful, perhaps one that speaks to them of peace. We must use whatever we find most helpful. Whatever you choose, use it to lead your mind into quietness. As it is usually more difficult to bring the mind to rest than it is the body, you should not be discouraged if it requires persistence. At your first times of prayer, you may get no further than the attempt to arrive at tranquillity, but in time both body and mind come to a measure of quietness. Some people, on the other hand, fall asleep as they relax. This shows their need of release from tension. Should they sleep there need be no sense of guilt. It is for them a necessary phase and it will pass as the practice of this form of prayer has the effect of making them more relaxed people. Remain in the quietness of body and mind for a short time.

Stage 4. Awareness of God

Now to direct the attention to God. He is within. So our loving attention can be given to Him there. We concentrate our heart and mind on to Him so that our whole desire is to be with Him. To keep our attention on God we may repeat His name slowly, quietly or silently. Use the name that is more natural–God, Father, Lord, Jesus, Spirit. Repeat this name as the attention is gently held on God without strain. Now, in the silence of the heart, be with God. Rest in Him. Ask nothing and seek nothing but to be one with Him and allow Him to reveal His presence to you. As He does you may in your heart adore and love Him. But the important thing is that you are with your God solely for the reason of being with Him and that there you remain, repeating His name as you feel necessary. This is the centre of all true prayer.

Stage 5. Receiving His life

Now put yourself into His hands. Open up the whole of your life to Him. Release God into every part of your being. Take Him into your thoughts, the good, the bad and the useless ones. Then into your emotions, the good and healthy ones and the unhealthy and damaging ones. Offer your relationships and again the good, the indifferent and the disturbing ones. Now receive Him into your inner life back to conception; into the pains and humiliations, the hurts and rejections, known and unknown. God knows all that has ever happened to you from conception and, as He is allowed freedom within, He will move in and do His healing and saving work. There is nothing He does not know and nothing He does not wish to share, forgive, heal and bless. So surrender your whole being to Him and have the peace of letting Him take over as you rest in His unchanging love. Finally let Him fill every cell of your body.

Stay with Him, face to face, in the silence. Rest in the presence of God. Be at one with Him and stay in that communion as long as you desire to or are able.

As we continue this form of prayer each day, we need have in mind only the movement of it. This is:

Be in a comfortable position.
Relax the body.
Quieten the mind.
Turn your loving attention on to God within.
Receive His life into your whole being.

In this relationship with God, we may then, if we wish, make our intercession. Having come into a real awareness of God, any intercession we make will have greater effect.

5

Some important considerations

The prayer of meeting God (or waiting upon Him) described in the previous chapter is the kind of prayer which leads us to want to be with Him in prayer. To rest in God, enjoy Him and receive His life within us as we do so, draws us in time to a constant awareness of life in communion with Him.

As we learn to meet God when we pray, a 'taste' for prayer will develop. That is, our spiritual appetite will be awakened and we will want to pray. This really means that we have developed a taste for God Himself, as the psalmist found, 'O taste and see that the Lord is good!' (34.8). Until we reach this point, our prayer will probably have a large element of duty about it. It is worth all the time and perseverance to get past duty to desires and taste. From this, the rich world of prayer opens up. The precise content of this world will depend to some extent upon each person's situation, but it will include knowing God with intimacy, experiencing the life of the kingdom of heaven as we are led into it, becoming aware of and learning to share the world of Spirit and silence, and entering into a process of change. What a joy it is as God changes us!

Is such prayer selfish?

It is sometimes maintained that this contemplative form of prayer is selfish because we are caring for ourselves and not praying for others. But contemplative prayer and intercessory prayer are not mutually exclusive. It was pointed out earlier that when we are in living touch with God, our intercession is more effective.

First it should be said that, as Paul teaches us in his second letter to the Corinthians, we should live our lives with our eyes constantly upon the world to come (4.16–5.10). There, presumably, the things we intercede for here will no longer apply but our life will be one of adoring God in company with the heavenly host. We shall live totally for God. So St Augustine's well-known words point us to this type of prayer, 'Thou hast made us for thyself and our hearts are restless till they find their rest in thee.' As we practise being with God in prayer and worshipping Him, we are preparing ourselves in the best way for the life to come.

It is, of course, possible to make any prayer selfish. Intercession can become a selfish pleading for what we want. We can turn any part of our religious life on to ourselves. But if we are genuinely close to God in prayer, it is inconceivable that He will allow it to become selfish. On the contrary, in this way of prayer we place ourselves in God's hands to do whatever is His will for us. We try to be totally open to Him. In time our greatest longing becomes the surrender of ourselves. We say, with John the Baptist, 'He must increase, but I must decrease' (John 3.30). So our desire is for God to make us usable and we can come to the point where our longing is, 'Do whatever you like with me, Lord.'

Feeling God's presence

We all like to feel the presence of God when we pray. This will be the case at times, but prayer is more than feeling and God does not allow us to live our prayer life by our feelings because this may lead us to want Him only for the nice things He does. God wants to teach us to want Him for Himself and to worship Him because He is Creator and Lord of all.

Therefore He will at times leave us with little or no sense of His presence so that we may learn to fix our attention on Him rather than on ourselves. If we co-operate with God when He withdraws the sense of His presence, we open the way for three things to happen. God will be able to test our love for Him; He will teach us to persevere, and He will strengthen our spiritual muscles as we keep on determinedly. These three things are essential if we are to mature in prayer.

If such is our intention, then, however our prayer is going each day, we can say to God, 'Well, Lord, if You wanted to, You could pour glorious delights of Yourself over me. If You are not doing so today, that is how You want it to be. Because You are love, what You are doing today is the very best for me.'

More will be said about this matter when discussing difficulties in prayer, but it is as well to point out here that, because of our changeable nature and circumstances, our prayer experience may not necessarily be the same two days running. If we realise this, it will ease any sense of disappointment we may feel at times.

God our Servant

The rich possibilities open to us in prayer by God's action can be ours because God is willing to be our Servant. So Jesus described Himself: 'For even the Son of Man did not come to be served; he came to serve and to give his life to redeem many people' (Mark 10.45, GNB). This is a mind-blowing revelation but it graphically indicates that God alone is able to do those things necessary to bring us to eternal life and to enable us to live in it. Only He, that is, can forgive us, give us rebirth, cleanse us from sin, graft us into Himself, apportion spiritual gifts and make the life of the kingdom of heaven possible to us. So He must serve us. Our prayer, therefore, has to be of a kind that frees Him to do these things in us. When we are at one with Him and open to Him in inner silence, we allow Him to carry out His redeeming work within us. He, of course, uses many other opportunities, but here we are seeing our relationship with Him from the standpoint of prayer.

So God will save us from attempting to use Him. He will lessen our desire for Him to change His purposes either for us personally or for the world generally. So, by His grace, the temptation to coax, wheedle or manipulate Him will lessen.

Silence in prayer

Earlier, we looked at our Lord's warning against

wordiness in prayer. As we learn to control this, we enter into the world of inner silence. Inner silence is more important than outer silence, for we can learn to preserve inner silence when we are surrounded by noise. And surrounded we are. Because we live in a world of noise with words bombarding us from all directions, it may not be easy at first to accustom ourselves to silence. We may feel ill at ease and restless. In time, however, a love of silence can grow for we shall find in it the rest, peace and satisfaction for which our souls long. In our relationship with God it is heart and will that matter. Words are not essential and may become a hindrance, for the profoundest experiences of personality defy such expression.

Further, the clamour around us can creep into us so that our minds and emotions become disturbed. Experiences in life and emotional suffering play their part also in causing inner agitation. Regular relaxation and rest in God bring a quietening to these disturbing influences. But God does more, His action within is a healing action and He will touch the sources of disturbance.

Silence will open a world of discovery of God and of ourselves. It is a mantle which enfolds us, holding us at one in God. It can be a world of acceptance and warmth where the soul is free to be itself and expand in its natural atmosphere as a flower opens in warm sunlight. As we are still and silent in God's presence, barriers come down between Him and us and He communicates with us. 'Spirit to spirit speaks' and we learn to recognise God, even though no words may describe Him.

In the accepting presence of God, emotions such as anger, fear, jealousy, bitterness and anxiety which so disturb us can become stilled. They do not suddenly evaporate, but they can be held by God so that they do not hinder our fellowship with Him. In the process of our prayer life as we rest in Him and allow Him freedom to act within us, part of His action is with these very emotions, which change slowly under His hand.

When we are quiet with God it also means that He is free to communicate with us. This may not be in words, but in His very active part of the relationship He will, when it is right, encourage us, guide, reveal or correct. Help can come for problems that worry us, He may give guidance, or lay upon us a burden for someone or something. If we teach, preach or write we may find that ideas will come into the mind. So it can be helpful to have pen and paper handy to note what the Lord may say. We have to learn to hear the Lord and, if necessary, to be willing to have our understanding tested. More will be said of this later.

Once we become accustomed to being in the silence with our Lord it will be for us the highest form of prayer fellowship with Him.

Meeting oneself

One of the results of this form of prayer is that we meet ourselves as well as God. This may not be the most pleasant of all experiences, for we must all have some things in our personalities which we would prefer to ignore. For people who have difficulty in accepting themselves, this can drive them into a more superficial form of prayer or even make them wish to cease from prayer altogether. But we are greatly strengthened in our spiritual and emotional growth if we hold ourselves into God, trusting that He truly accepts us and is waiting to deal with the very things which most disappoint us in ourselves.

On the other hand, when 'the veil is removed' between us and God, as Paul teaches us in 2 Corinthians 3.18: 'All of us, then, reflect the glory of the Lord with uncovered faces; and that same glory, coming from the Lord, who is the Spirit, transforms us into his likeness in an ever greater degree of glory' (GNB). This, of course, is the fundamental activity of God, because it is for this that He has made us. The process may be slow, but it does take place, and that fact should make us not be afraid to present ourselves to ourselves as well as to God in prayer.

As our relationship with God develops in prayer, part of the process of being changed into His likeness is the action of the Spirit in revealing our sin and the need of cleansing. When He does this there is no sense of condemnation, nor does He create in us any feeling of worthlessness. Rather, it is all part of the kingly work of God to raise us into richer communion with Him. God never speaks nor acts before we are able to respond and always He is positive. Hence, we do not need to ferret about within ourselves in order to winkle out our sins. This is a useless and damaging exercise. Nor should we attempt to make an assessment of ourselves for we are bound to be wrong. We can safely leave it all to the Holy Spirit to show us what He wants to show us and when. Our objective should be to 'die to ourselves' which means, among other things, moving towards being unaware of ourselves. What bliss! Such a revolution can be brought about by no one but God Himself.

God reveals Himself to each of us in a sovereign way. It may be that to someone in the early stages of the Christian life God may grant a rich experience of Himself. On the other hand, a mature Christian of many years' faithful service may receive little or no evidence of God's presence through spiritual 'consolations', as the contemplative writers call them. Neither case should cause pride or disappointment. God is not more nor less present within each. It means that He does what is best for us at each particular stage of our spiritual pilgrimage. Provided, therefore, that our will is, as far as we may make it, at one with God, we should rest content with whatever He chooses to do in His wisdom and love. The 'dry' periods can mean that we are in a process of maturing. It is by persevering when there seems little reward for doing so, that our love for God is most clearly shown. In such a situation praying in tongues can prove a boon and encouragement.

Those who develop this interior relationship with God become aware in time of His constant presence within. Perhaps this is because prayer has become a love relationship. We desire God and wish to be constantly with Him, while He delights to give Himself to us and to share in our living. God is then a natural and essential part of life, not merely someone to be called upon in need, but to be enjoyed. Charles Wesley expressed this admirably in the words,

For thee delightfully employ
   Whate'er thy bounteous grace hath given,
And run my course with even joy,
   And closely walk with thee to heaven.

The whole hymn is an expressive description of a life lived in constant awareness of God.

It seems, too, that it results in a simplification of life. Almost without our realising it, the Spirit works within, gradually drawing together all aspects of our life, so that our entire life is an expression of God's will for us. So thoughts, life style, habits, interests, activities and relationships tend to cohere. Our aim is for our life to become so disciplined that we also can say of our lives what our Lord said of His life with His Father, 'I always do what pleases him' (John 8.29). For us, such an aim is inevitably a life-long one but, as we develop, so does our potential.

Prayer is many-sided

Learning to enter into the relaxed inner meeting with God described earlier does not exclude other natural or taught ways of praying. Two or more ways may go along together as they are needed—daily offices, devotional acts and prayers, meditation on the Bible and, at times, praying aloud. Some find prayer is evoked by nature's beauty, others that prayer comes easily when walking. Our aim should be to have as rich and varied a life in God as possible and the Holy Spirit who is the Lord and giver of life will help us.

6

Intercessory prayer

The prayer of meeting with God which we have tried to describe in Chapter 4 does not mean that intercession is unnecessary. But we do have to take care that it does not become the only form of prayer that we offer to God or even that it become the dominant part. Prayer which consists only or mainly of asking for things hardly does justice to our faith nor gives glory to God.

It cannot be over-emphasised that the heart of prayer must be the worship and adoration of God and we should make the habit of putting this first when we pray. If we do this and open ourselves to God at the same time, as has been described, then the life of God flows into us. Thus, to quote Paul's words in the graphic translation of J. B. Phillips, 'Already we have the love of God flooding through our hearts by the Holy Spirit given to us' (Rom. 5.5). That love will activate our hearts, making us more aware of needs and so it will issue in prayer for them.

So intercessory prayer will be a valid and necessary part of our Christian life. It is the form of prayer which comes to us most naturally, since usually it is the first kind of prayer we learn as children, and we fly to it whenever we have a strong need. Much public worship includes it and it has plenty of biblical authority. It is also in the plan of God in that He appears to restrict Himself deliberately in order to depend to some extent upon our prayer co-operation for the working out of His will. Our prayer, that is to say, releases His action. It is a privilege so to be allowed to share in God's work.

Jesus, in the Lord's Prayer, gives us a guide for our intercession. The first part is concerned with God Himself and with the working out of His will on earth; the second with ourselves and our needs. It is instructive to recognise what our Lord sees these needs to be. They are for daily food, for forgiveness, for help in temptation and for deliverance from evil. These are our basic needs, physical and spiritual. Unless God meets these needs, a human being cannot survive as a whole person.

Our intercession, therefore, should be based upon a clear appreciation of our Lord's teaching. We will, clearly, have a wide variety of needs deriving from these primary ones, but we should try to remember the main thrust of the Lord's Prayer which is the bringing about of God's will on earth. We pray for God to meet our needs in order to make us able to co-operate with Him in that work.

This teaching of Jesus can also be seen as a description of God Himself if we express the elements of it as statements about God rather than as requests.

God is your Father.
He reigns in the glory of heaven.
His name is to be hallowed,
His will is to be done on earth
  as it is in heaven.
He gives you each day your daily bread;
He forgives you your sins;
He does not lead you into temptation,
but He delivers you from evil.

This is a magnificent picture of God which can fill us with confidence in Him. It is in our confidence in such a caring God that we rest and make our requests.

To intercede means 'to act or plead on behalf of another'. It is 'standing by someone' and that is part of the work of the Holy Spirit. Jesus called Him the Paraclete, that is 'He who comes to our aid', 'He who stands by us'. Our intercession should, then, be 'in the Holy Spirit'.

Paul teaches us this in his letter to the Romans. He says, 'Likewise the Spirit helps us in our weakness; for we do not know how to pray as we ought, but the Spirit Himself intercedes for us with sighs too deep for words. And he who searches the hearts of men knows what is the mind of the Spirit, because the Spirit intercedes for the saints according to the will of God (8.26–7).

In that passage Paul says that we do not know how to pray as we should but that the Holy Spirit does. He, fortunately, is interceding for and with us. Paul emphasises two aspects of the Holy Spirit's prayer which differentiate it from our own. First, He is praying at a depth beyond our understanding, agonising, it seems, in the situation, and secondly, His intercession is totally in harmony with the will of God. What encouragement it gives to have the Holy Spirit involved with our prayer.

Since we are not alone in our prayer we should put ourselves into the hands of the Spirit when we intercede, asking Him to take our prayer and use it His way. As a result, He may change the way we are praying or He may provide a different answer. Because of this, and also when it is difficult to know just how to pray in a situation, many people pray in tongues. As the Spirit gives the tongue, it can then truly be His prayer. This can reduce any selfish element in our praying and any tendency to be inward looking.

Intercession means that others need us. No one is sufficient of himself. Even our Lord could ask, 'Could you not watch with me one hour?' and Paul constantly, it seems, asked for prayer—'Brethren, pray for us.' We also need others and it is a source of true strength and encouragement when we can trust people to stand with us in prayer at a time of need. Intercession binds us together in the body of Christ in a fellowship of support, compassion and suffering. It may well issue in action, for the Lord will want us to be involved in our prayer and so may call us to be the one whom He uses for the answer.

A method of intercession

While intercession can be a very personal matter and we form our own way of praying, the following may be a useful guide or open up some helpful point.

a. First spend time unhurriedly to be at one with God in order to be aware of being in touch with Him.

b. Remember that Jesus is already with those for whom we pray: 'As you did it to one of the least of these my brethren, you did it to me' (Matt. 25.40). See Jesus with them, standing by them and caring for them infinitely more than we can.

c. But also, if we truly care, that person or need is, as we say, 'on our heart'. Our Lord is also in our heart as well as being with the person or situation, wherever that may be. So we link both together in our heart. We hold them into Christ and His grace then works in the person or situation.

d. It helps to know as much about the need as we can, for this can evoke our compassion. Compassion was the source of our Lord's caring ministry (Matt. 9.36).

e. We can then open our whole being to the Holy Spirit and let Him lead the prayer. We should hold our attention on to God as it is His action that matters. His life can then flow through us to the need. As indicated earlier, we should be attentive to the Holy Spirit should He wish to influence our prayer.

f. It helps to make our prayer as positive as we can. We may use such an approach as, 'Thank You, Father, that You are fully involved in this situation and are now at work in it according to Your perfect love and wisdom.' So we can continue to hold the person or situation into God as we feel necessary under the Spirit.

It is sometimes asserted that we need to pray only once for any need because God does not forget. It is quite true that He doesn't, but it is a misunderstanding of intercessory prayer to speak in this way. Prayer is more than making a request. The out-working of God's response through our co-operation is essential and this continues as we hold it before God. So we remain God's channel for as long as there is a need.

One aspect of this is supportive prayer. For certain needs our prayer is an ongoing one perhaps for years. Such examples of this need are parents for their children, and prayer for missionaries and for other parts of the continuing work of the Church. Christians and others suffering under Communist and Rightist regimes need this persistent supportive prayer.

But we cannot pray for everyone! The demand for prayer can become a burden and the process of going through long lists is a boring experience for some, even though prayers may be apportioned daily over a period. It is as well to remember that only God can care for the whole world and He does not ask us to do all His work for Him. So we should select carefully, trying to be guided by the Holy Spirit. We should at times check what has happened as a result of prayer and pass on to other situations and people.

Because of this vast need and of each person's ability to touch only the fringe, some people curtail their specific intercession to a very small number of needs which they feel God is putting on their hearts. Much of their prayer is then offered to God so that He may use it as He wishes. Thus, when in prayer with God as described in Chapter 4, they remain attentively with Him offering Him their prayer. They say, in effect, 'Lord, I am offering this prayer to You. Use it for whoever You choose or in whatever way You know to be best.' They then remain with God confident that their prayer is being used in the best possible way. There is much satisfaction in doing this as the burden is taken off their shoulders and they can have perfect trust in God's use of the prayer.

Intercession need not be carried out only during our specific quiet time, but whenever opportunity presents itself. Some people have a special time of day for intercession. Others find help in having photographs about the house and pray for each as they pass. One common habit is to hold people into Christ when doing monotonous jobs or at certain fixed times during the day. We can each work out our own method according to our personality, routine and circumstances.

7

Along the way

One of the pitfalls about prayer is to departmentalise it. That is, we treat it as one of the many things we do which make up our lives and confine it to set prayer times. There is not much prayer growth that way. We should pray so that God can become involved in our lives. Hence prayer and life are to be seen as one whole. One part of this is our ability to hear God, for unless we do, prayer is one-sided and God does not direct our lives. So we should learn to listen to Him.

Listening to God

Every one of us who is a sincere Christian has as his aim to live close to God and to become the person He intends us to be. It follows that we will wish to know God's will for ourselves both in the process of inner change and for the course of our life. Thus listening to God—being aware of what He is saying and doing—becomes an integral part of life as we live with Him.

With such an attitude to God, we will do our best

to live open to Him. Perhaps much that we receive may not be recognised as such, but will do its work unnoticed within us. There may be others who are disappointed because they feel God does not speak to them. In their case it may be that they are thinking too narrowly and it may help them to widen their view. In the words of Keble's poem they could pray:

Give me a heart to find out thee,
And read thee everywhere.

It should help us if we remember that we live in a sacramental universe. That is, God 'comes through' His creation and will reveal Himself to those who are looking for Him. Paul has pointed this out to us: 'Ever since the creation of the world his invisible nature, namely, his eternal power and deity, has been clearly perceived in the things that have been made' (Rom. 1.20). We have to learn to become sensitive to God's word in whatever way it comes to us and we can train ourselves to look for it in creation, in Scripture, in suffering, through conversation, in our reading, worship and prayer. When God is truly speaking to us we recognise Him and so can receive what He says and allow it to work in us.

The charismatic renewal has awakened an increasing number of people to the possibility that God will speak. This is being discovered particularly in the caring ministries. We find that His word comes to us during a conversation, when sharing someone's problem or suffering or when counselling. Or an idea is popped into the mind when we are on the telephone, on a visit or when writing a letter. Similarly, when in prayer, a burden comes upon us to pray for somebody or a situation and then all else gives way to this pressure from God. The rediscovery of the gifts of the Spirit has revolutionised this whole area of listening to God, and we are encouraged to have a more positive approach to ministry as we see God compensating for our own inadequacy.

It is an encouragement when we have responded to such a touch of God to ourselves or for others, just as it is when we have recognised a work of His in our lives. Sometimes, however, it seems that we have misheard God. This does not necessarily follow, for it may be that others involved have not co-operated with what God was doing. But if we do make a mistake this must not dishearten us. Listening to God is not easy and we all make mistakes. This can be painfully evident when what we have thought God has said does not happen or when the 'guidance' turns out to be wrong. Our 'failure' may also come the other way round in that there seems to be no response at all from God though we are open to Him and long to hear from Him.

There are no easy answers to such dilemmas because learning to listen to God is a lifetime's occupation. Nevertheless we should all be hoping to receive enrichment to our lives and ministry by the activity of God and so should make it an adventure to learn to be perceptive to Him. It must be God's will to communicate with us and to enrich us and so listening to Him should be seen as a normal part of our co-operation with Him. The more our prayer develops the more able we shall be to discern what God is doing.

Guidance

Listening to God is obviously a very large factor in receiving guidance from Him. Those involved in the pastoral ministry are only too well aware that receiving guidance is a perennial problem. It should give us all encouragement to know that not only for all of us is it difficult but that it was, at times at least, not all that easy for our Lord. He had to spend forty days and nights in the wilderness wrestling out how He was to fulfil His mission. Satan used the flesh, Jesus' divine powers and the ultimate end of all His work in an attempt to turn our Lord away from discerning and accepting the Father's will. In the same way, when we are seeking God's will it may be a battle and be some time before blockages of self are overcome and we can hear God clearly. On another occasion the choosing of the Twelve meant for Christ a whole night in prayer with His Father. It should not surprise us therefore if we do not get an immediate answer ourselves.

The following comments are made in the hope that where they apply they may provide some yardstick for ascertaining the will of God. It will do no harm to say at the outset that asking guidance for something we dearly desire will itself almost certainly make it more difficult for us to hear God's voice. Our very desire will cloud our hearing. It is then so easy to let a text from the Bible, a bit of a prophecy, circumstances and snippets of conversation to act as confirmation of the guidance we want. In such an instance the clearing away of our own desires can be a demanding experience. Contrariwise, to contemplate an answer from God which will mean hardship, sacrifice or suffering equally calls for a dying to self. These remarks are not intended to convey that God wants to give us only hard and unpleasant things, but merely to encourage us to be realistic about our difficult human nature.

If we mention first the guidance of our life as a whole—how we work out God's overall will for us—then we can be quite confident that, provided we are determined that following God's purpose for us is our fundamental reason for living, He will get us where He wants us. Even if we frustrate His action at points in our lives God will be like the other one at a game of chess. He will counteract our moves, knowing the end He has in mind for us into eternity. If we put ourselves as far as we honestly can into His hands, then 'in everything God works for good with those who love him' (Rom. 8.28).

One basic principle, which we must always apply when seeking for guidance, is that it will never be against the general teaching of the Bible. For example, one has in the past seen the following text quoted as authority to leave the Church and call people out to form a separate group—'Wherefore come out from among them, and be ye separate, saith the Lord' (2 Cor. 6.17 AV). However, Paul is speaking here about the marriage of Christians with unbelievers. Further, the broad teaching of the Scriptures is poignantly expressed by our Lord in what is called the High Priestly Prayer of Jesus in John 17: '. . . that they may all be one; even as thou, Father, art in me, and I in thee, that they may be in us' (v. 21). This expresses the teaching of every book of the New Testament about the unity of Christians in the body of Christ. Anyone can separate themselves in order to go their own way. It takes much more grace and discipline to stay and learn to live with others who do not think as we do.

The experience of the Church as a whole may also be a guide to our particular situation. In the Church through the ages Christians have had to learn how to follow God. We learn both by their correct decisions and by their mistakes, for many of the same sort of problems face Christians in every age.

It should also be realised that the Holy Spirit will not tell us what to do if we are capable of discovering this ourselves. As we mature as Christians our understanding deepens, and as part of this process the Spirit teaches us to use what we have learnt already. If therefore we are waiting upon God for guidance and nothing apparently comes, we should first ask ourselves if God is saying, 'You can work it out yourself.' Neither should we ignore common sense and our down to earth experience of life. Some people seem to have a facility for making the word 'spiritual' mean 'irrational'.

But moments come when we genuinely do not know what we should do. In such circumstances God must lead us. It can help us to arrive at a decision if we list all the 'fors' and 'againsts'. We should first write down the various factors for and against. Then do the same with our motives, hopes and fears. This clears the mind and helps us eliminate or wrestle against the factors which would cloud the hearing of God's voice. Then if we patiently wait upon the Lord daily, His will can come through.

There are other helps in finding the will of God. One is to ask whether what we propose would please God. This was axiomatic in the life of our Lord. He said of His Father, 'I always do what is pleasing to him' (John 8.29). Paul similarly teaches us to live 'to please God' (1 Thess. 4.1). Undoubtedly our understanding of what pleases God will change from time to time, and sometimes we may even be mistaken. But if we truly want to please God we will be living close to Him and He will be able to influence us. Another help is to ask the opinion of one or more mature people who care enough about us to tell us what they really think. God can also speak to us through the Bible, and a sense of peace may signify that the decision taken is the right one. Some have followed Gideon in putting out a 'fleece' before God. That is, they say to Him, 'If this is your will, would you confirm it by making such and such happen?' Others have at times 'pushed doors' and if an approach has opened a way, they have accepted that as God's will.

If we are requiring guidance for a matter of some import, it is wise to seek confirmation from more than one of these sources. God does not object to our returning to Him for confirmation, neither does He hurry. The devil will want to rush us into a wrong decision but God has all eternity and acts calmly and unhurriedly. If, on our part, we truly wish to hear God's word to us, we will gladly test what we feel in as many ways as seems necessary.

The experience of Christians indicates that God's ways of guiding us may change as we move through life. He may need to teach us different things at different times. His direction may come with clarity at one time while at another we may be called to take a step in faith which God confirms in various ways as we follow what we are trusting to be God's will. It is the experience of some that as they have grown in knowledge and experience of God, His guidance has not come in the obvious ways it came when they were young in the faith.

A quite different way of finding God's will is used by some Christians. They first discuss the matter until they come to a common mind which they then accept as the will of God. Then they use prayer to pray the decision through to fulfilment.

Listening to God and being guided by Him are all part of our quest for God and His life. But clearly, if we are to hear God speak we must learn how to hear. So it is most important that we should improve our ability to be silent and attentive before Him in prayer. Not only this, but being able to rest in God in prayer also means that we can quieten any inner disturbance which may be evoked by the need to make an important decision. The voice of God will then be able to come through.

This last point of resting in God in prayer leads to another way in which God 'speaks' to us. This is by imprinting Himself upon our soul. As we learn to wait upon God and look at Him face to face we receive Him into ourselves, as a camera receives the light waves which form the picture. There may be no 'message' or picture but He is bringing Himself into direct association with our inner self and we are receiving His life. This subtle 'speaking' may seem intangible but it is a powerful way in which God communicates Himself to us.

Prayer and life generally

Learning to hear God's voice in our lives is one part of our walk along the spiritual road. It is an essential part, for God must guide us into our life in the kingdom of heaven, every step of which is a step into the unknown. One of the arresting revelations of God in the Bible is that He is a God who speaks to direct and teach His people. We see this from Abraham onwards.

In order to learn to hear God, we must arrange our daily life so that our prayer can have a strong effect upon it. This effect must be powerful enough to counteract and overcome the voices and temptations which try to insinuate themselves into us from many directions. This means that we will constantly turn our minds to God and seek to be close to Him in our daily life. Throughout the day we will long for God, we will set our hearts upon Him, and will affirm that we are made for Him and that He wants us. The unfolding of such a union will be the adventure of our lives. It is an adventure which is an eternal one and, because of the infinite glory of God, it will never cease to satisfy and thrill us.

Such is the vision God gives to the soul. It is essential to keep this vision before our eyes because our own weakness and the vagaries of life may cloud it so that, at times, it is by our will alone that we keep on. One of the golden rules of much of the living of our life in Christ is, 'Keep on going on'.

Our desire for God means we want to be like Him. We want the barriers caused by sin, ignorance and our fallen human nature to crumble so that the process of conforming to Christ may proceed. The words of Paul in Romans 12 ring clear to a soul in this hopeful condition, 'I appeal to you therefore, brethren, by the mercies of God, to present your bodies as a living sacrifice, holy and acceptable to God, which is your spiritual worship. Do not be conformed to this world but be transformed by the renewal of your mind, that you may prove what is the will of God, what is good and acceptable and perfect' (12.1–2). Paul goes on to elaborate life in the kingdom of God as it relates to our estimation of ourselves, being part of the body of Christ, generally, and specifically to our personal relationships. Even a superficial reading of his words makes us see clearly that we must depend completely upon God if such a quality of life is to be our own. Thankfully we remember other words of Paul: 'It is God who works in you to will and to act according to his good purpose' (Phil. 2.13, NIV).

It is because of that that we can put ourselves into his hands and depend on him; and it is this that enables God 'to will and to act according to his good purpose'. Knowing this, we can from our side foster a genuine co-operation between God and ourselves. We can then be in a hopeful state of heart and face daily life in the confidence that we are not alone—God is with us.

This realisation of the continuing presence of God within and around us can have a radical effect upon our daily living. With Christ free to move within us our personality and character traits will be transformed. It will mostly happen unconsciously. Perhaps we are most likely to be aware of this glorious work when we recognise that some aspect of our behaviour or the way we react to a situation has undergone a change for the better. For example, our growing sensitivity to our Lord's presence through prayer must condition our inner thoughts. If we are aware that Christ's eyes as well as our own are focused upon our thoughts, it is much more difficult to harbour those which would not please Him. This also applies to our habits, relationships, work, prejudices, reading, viewing and recreation. Our conscience will become more sensitive and our criteria of life will improve. So there will be a more positive striving against the less desirable parts of ourselves. Through it all we shall thankfully appreciate the faithfulness of God. No failure or disobedience on our part drives Him away.

Our own striving is, of course, only one side of this work. The greater part is the work of God within us—what we call God's grace. All of us have varying success in our attempts to draw upon God's help, in our ability to withstand the attraction of certain sins and to muster our strength and will as we walk this road in the kingdom of heaven. Gloriously we serve a God 'whose nature is always to have mercy' and to forgive, and so we live our days in His forgiving love. Our failures must not dishearten us: 'If God is for us, who can be against us?' (Rom. 8.31, GNB). We may also add, 'What can be against us?' Our Lord is not one 'who is unable to sympathise with our weaknesses, but one who in every respect has been tempted as we are' (Heb. 4.15). He realises well enough that we, unlike Him, are not without sin, and so He is ready and 'able to help those who are tempted' (Heb. 2.18). Our Lord, then, will see to it that there are encouragements along the way, the greatest being the sweetness of His companionship. It is this undergirding in our Christian journey which comes through prayer.

A word must be said for the people who, because of wrong biblical teaching or as a result of emotional damage, believe God to be a demanding taskmaster whose standard they can never reach and whom they fear rather than love. The notion that such a God sees all can be alarming. It is a case of 'Big Brother is watching you'. One has deep sympathy for such people for, if this conception is well ingrained, they are caught between a desire to escape from such a Being, and a fear of disobedience. No spiritual life can flourish in such circumstances. Even if the concept is not severe, there is still some unwillingness to have close association with such a God, and so prayer is inhibited.

The healing of such a false idea will almost certainly demand individual help, particularly if the cause is due to emotional mishandling at some period. It may well be that all cases have some emotional content. This condition can be rectified by good counselling. But it must also be remembered that the Holy Spirit is the Spirit of truth and it is part of His work to dispel mistaken belief. If, therefore, anyone suffering from such an idea of God will cling faithfully to Him, and by act of will trust in a God who loves and saves, the Holy Spirit will find a way to set him free. Patience may be needed, but the Spirit will do His work till the moment of change comes. Taking God into the inner life back to conception, in the way that has already been described, will offer the Spirit the opening for such healing.

If prayer affects our life, then the way we live has a bearing on our prayer. As has been pointed out already, discipline of spirit, mind and heart are necessary for alert and fruitful prayer. It follows that self-indulgence in our way of life will work against prayer discipline. So we should aim at a sensibly controlled way of life. This does not entail asceticism. Rather it calls for wise restraint in food, drink, use of our time and enough (but not too much) sleep. To present our bodies as a living sacrifice, holy and acceptable to God, is not a burden to those who want God, neither is it a miserable self-denial. On the contrary, one feels much fitter and more alert when such control is exercised. Inevitably this leads to alertness in prayer.

Our inner life must also come under examination. In our life with God we should co-operate with the

Holy Spirit to achieve the cleansing and ordering of our thoughts and attitudes. Should these be contrary to God they weaken our desire for Him. The real problem here is that, unless we take positive steps to allow the Spirit into this inner area, we remain at a level which neither sees nor longs for a vital relationship with God. We opt for an unproductive meander with God which is disappointing and causes a mild sense of guilt because we have not faced up to the demand for change. It is only by an act of will and a steady perseverance in responding to God's challenge that we rise above this state. We need to beg God's grace for this to happen. Fortunately His longing for us is greater than ours for Him, and so we can be sure that He will be working to bring us to Himself.

We need also to pay attention to our emotional condition. Anxiety, inner agitation, insecurity, depression, despondency, guilt and feeling we are unlovable are some of the distressing states which can eat at our peace of mind and spirit and undermine our zest for life. In the more serious instances there seems no freedom from them. We may become thoroughly disheartened because no matter how hard we try, these disorders do not lose their power. In such circumstances help should be sought from someone competent to release the inner pain and heal the damage. This condition, also, should be used as a spur to prayer that God will enter into the pain areas and continue His healing there. Many have been healed in this way. Light emotional problems do not necessarily prove damaging to the prayer life for they expose a need for God but are not severe enough to produce spiritual inertia.

Our life is one whole and so no part can be dissociated from the rest. What is good and positive can be developed so that the less agreeable diminishes. We should follow John the Baptist who could say of his relationship with Christ, 'He must increase, I must decrease.' As the awareness of Christ increases in us, so, thankfully, all parts of our life come under His influence. Prayer and life fuse into one because prayer becomes a constant state of heart. The masters of the spiritual life have called this a state of 'recollection'. This means that our relationship with God is continuous even though our attention may, quite rightly, be on such things as work, recreation or service. It is rather like an intimate human relationship which is always part of our lives, no matter what we may actually be doing when we are apart.

Fasting

A word here may be said about fasting, for at times when the intervention of God is essential, fasting has been found to be a helpful weapon.

Fasting helps in that it makes us able to be alert both mentally and spiritually. Abstinence from food eliminates the sleepiness that a full stomach produces. It means also that we intend business. We are prepared to take steps to co-operate with God and so facilitate His action. When something important is at stake, as when someone is critically ill, or in danger; when we are facing strong temptation or have to make an important decision, or in action against evil powers, all the forces of our prayer may be necessary. So we may feel called by the Spirit to undergird our prayer with fasting.

In learning to fast, we should start by missing one meal. That is not too much for any of us. Then we can increase the period without food, but with a sensible awareness of what is possible for us. When they fast, most people do not include abstinence from liquids, though they may take only water or fruit juice. Coffee and tea can be discontinued gradually over a few days before the fast begins to eliminate caffeine withdrawal symptoms. As the body is able to exist without food for some weeks, a day or two's fast can produce only benefit to our bodies. Such effects as headache and smelly breath can be ignored for they do no harm to us. It should, perhaps, be pointed out that to have a large meal before fasting only makes the discontinuance of food more difficult. Small meals prior to the time of fasting help most, for the body begins to demand less nourishment.

The Holy Spirit is bringing back to us the need to fast in certain circumstances. It is well to have this weapon in mind when we meet a demanding situation. We should, however, understand that fasting is not only for emergencies. The renewal movement has alerted us to a new appreciation of it, but the Church has always encouraged us to fast. The Book of Common Prayer and the Alternative Service book both lay down rules for it. These rules apply to fasting as a regular practice undertaken to strengthen individual spiritual growth and form a Church effective under God to fulfil its function in the world. We need to be reminded that in such precious times as Lent, fasting is more than giving up some little thing. The discipline of refraining from all food at specific times has a place in our Christian lives. By practising it, we experience its effect on our love for God, our understanding of the Christian life and our times of prayer.

8

Struggles and difficulties in prayer

Prayer is an adventure into God. We should therefore practise it as positively and with as much enthusiasm as we can. It is also an art and like all arts there is much to learn and in learning we have problems, frustrations and failures. As in any art form, these difficulties should be regarded as challenges. So, though we have to be honest about the problems, we do not have to be dismal.

In prayer we are seeking God Himself and He wants to give us Himself. This receiving of what we are seeking leads us on day by day and makes the life of prayer a constant exploration. No worthwhile exploration is an untroubled, uneventful enterprise. Who would be satisfied with such a thing? Nor should we be with our prayer. But it is sensible to be aware of problems so that we may come to grips with them when they arise.

Prayer struggles

It is unlikely, and undesirable, that our prayer should continue in an untroubled sameness. Activity by the

Spirit within our spirits, as well as external happenings in our lives, will stop us settling into complacency. A living relationship with God is an eventful experience of sharing His redeeming work and of our own maturing in the process.

Paul warns us in his letter to the Galatians that 'The desires of the flesh are against the Spirit, and the desires of the Spirit are against the flesh; for these are opposed to each other' (5.17). As such is the case, the Holy Spirit will be in action where the flesh is opposing His work. He will, for example, act when we are tempted to put off our prayer time, and He will join with us in our struggle until together we win the battle and can get down to praying. For some, it can be a demanding battle and has to be fought out often until a daily habit is strongly formed.

Other struggles come at points where our nature conflicts with the life of the kingdom of heaven. Where our thoughts and habits, or our attitude towards such things as anxiety or self-indulgence, conflict with the life to which we have been called, the Holy Spirit will challenge us and activate our conscience.

The experience of many is that at the first such movement of the Spirit they push away the unwelcome idea. However, it has a habit of cropping up when reading the Bible or in sermons, books or conversation and so presses upon us. If we resist strongly it may seem to go away for a time, but if the Spirit is at work it inevitably returns just when we are least expecting it.

And so the fight is on. We wrestle with God and do our best to justify ourselves, but there is no peace until we accept what the Spirit is saying to us. Even then the struggle may not be over, for the wrong attitude or habit is not necessarily changed permanently and so the temptation can return. In this process we have to turn to God in contrition and with a clear awareness of our weakness. So God teaches us to throw ourselves upon His grace and, in surrender to Him, allow Him to work within until He has fulfilled His purpose.

Battles like this can go on for a long time and here again it is our daily prayer discipline which carries us through, for it means that we consistently place ourselves under the hand of God who in time breaks the power of the attraction. He does more. He creates a desire for the kingdom's life and that is the final defeat of the flesh. So we can move more closely into being one with God.

Paul warns us that we also meet the opposition of evil spirit forces, 'the wiles of the devil' (Eph. 6.11). Though some may be involved in an open fight with evil as, for example, in casting out evil spirits, for most people the activity of evil forces is experienced in more subtle ways, as they cause doubt and despondency, or bring about a lack of desire to pray or read the Bible. The call to put on the whole armour of God, to 'pray at all times in the Spirit, with all prayer and supplication', and to 'keep alert with all perseverance' (v. 18) is a salutary one. When we do that we follow our Lord who, in a different context, warned us, 'What I say to you I say to all: Watch'

(Mark 13.37). This state of spiritual alertness demands a regular daily prayer time.

At times things happen which matter so much that we are driven to agonise in prayer. These are times when our life feels that it will fall apart or when heart-breaking things happen to those who mean most to us, or when bereavement comes. Then we can feel helpless, bewildered and shattered. We pray hard and we keep on praying, for this situation mesmerises us and we cannot get it out of our mind. Our prayer is filled with it, however much we try to turn our minds to God. Perhaps after a time we feel a little easier because of our prayer. But soon the old feelings and the agony return and fear may clutch at our heart. So we plead to God again. In some cases it seems that at the very time when God's help is so badly needed, He is farthest away and the feeling of desolation and even despair can be great. This is a puzzling situation. Maybe the answer depends upon the individual personality, or perhaps the very intensity of need acts as a barrier to God.

Our response in such a situation will clearly depend upon the sort of person we are. We may plead and plead and try to twist God's arm or we may fall into depression, lose faith and even become bitter against God.

In a different situation, should our heart be aching for someone we love deeply, we may wish to bear the pain for them and we pray along those lines. Parents may feel this for their children and it is a natural reaction, but if this would lead to keeping the child in immaturity, the Lord will not answer that prayer.

There can be instances where we are called actually to take the pain of another, but experience suggests that this comes only as the result of a direct leading of God.

In such deeply disturbing circumstances, some may be able to take a philosophic attitude. The suffering may be offered back to God with such words as 'All things come from You, and of Your own do I give You.' Then the whole problem is left in the hands of God. Or the Holy Spirit may reveal that there is no quick solution and that what is called for is faithful prayer and trust that God has it all in hand and will work His will in due course.

Some, at least in certain situations, are even able to praise God. This is done in the faith that nothing is outside the Lord's influence and power and so, by an act of positive faith and praise, the whole matter is opened up to God's action. Some have been able to pray in this way even in great distress of heart. It is also possible to bear deep suffering by seeing it in its eternal context. Prayer is therefore made in terms of Paul's words in Romans 8, 'I consider that the sufferings of this present time are not worth comparing with the glory that is to be revealed to us' (v. 18). The same recognition is expressed in the words of Christ to Julian of Norwich, 'All shall be well, and all manner of thing shall be well.'

Perhaps most of us see our times of anguish as our part in the Cross. Jesus' cry of frustration, 'How often would I have gathered your children together . . . and you would not' (Matt. 23.37) find an echo in our own hearts because of our own unanswered longing. Even more, perhaps, His cry, 'My God, my God, why . . . ?' is the cry in our own tormented heart. In all He had to face, Jesus could go on, trusting His Father and determined at all costs to do His will. So we may go along such a road, with no immediate answer but knowing that Christ is involved with the external situation and with our prayer and longing as we co-operate with His unseen action.

This can be a true way of suffering with Christ. Because we believe He is totally involved in whatever causes our anguish it is as much His pain as ours. In this way we may find the peace He promised. We can remember that this promise was given a few hours before His life was to end in fearful torture, rejection and seeming failure. His own peace of heart was possible because of His being in total obedience to His Father, whatever the outcome. So the peace He offers us is one that emanates not from an untroubled existence but from the centre of suffering. Somehow in our own agonising we can ask Christ to lead us into His peace. As we pray in this way, we look forward to the new life that will follow the pain.

While none of us welcomes the painful times, they can lead us into sharing the life of God in prayer at a depth which may not be possible otherwise. His grace given to us may give us the strength to face such opportunities when they arise.

Difficulties in prayer

We should now turn our attention to some of the difficulties which all of us have to meet as we learn to pray. We will try to look at them positively so that by grappling with them we may make spiritual growth.

Wandering thoughts

This is the commonest difficulty one meets. It seems that no one ever becomes entirely free from them and it helps to accept that fact, rather than to become irritated with ourselves and disheartened. In accepting them we can quietly deal with them. That is, when we find that our thoughts are far away from God, we bring our attention *gently* back to Him. In this way we may continue our prayer without losing either our temper or our inner peace. This approach results in the least hindrance to prayer.

Wandering thoughts are, however, a rather more complicated matter than is sometimes realised. If we pay attention to the causes which we recognise, then we can do something to alleviate the problem. Here are some of possible causes:

a. Poor concentration. If our ability to concentrate is generally not good, it will not be good with prayer either. Even so, many people find that though they have reasonably good concentration normally, their thoughts can fly off in all sorts of directions when they pray. So we should do all we can to improve our concentration, and persist in trying to control our attention when in prayer. As our awareness of God grows stronger so there is a stronger focus for attention.

b. If our prayer is infrequent it will make concentration more difficult, just as it will make prayer growth unlikely.

c. Tiredness will make concentration difficult. We should try to find the cause of it. Such things as an undisciplined life, anxiety or over-busyness may be a cause. Tiredness can be a problem if we make our prayer time at the end of the day.
d. Emotional distractions such as grief, depression or inner disturbance will draw our thoughts away from God. Similarly scruple, despondency, cares and worries, and disturbing news can be like gnats buzzing around in our minds. They make it hard for us to hold our attention on to God.
e. We should constantly remember that we are not machines. For any number of reasons we vary from day to day and we should make allowances for this. Some days we have to accept that because of the situation prayer is going to be difficult.

'Dry' periods

These are times when there is little or no awareness of the presence of God. Any of the above causes of inattention may be a factor, but one common reason is unrepented sin. This will inevitably put a barrier between God and us for we will be in a state of guilt. This is not the case when temptation comes and we grapple with it. Even though the temptation may be so strong that it almost mesmerises us, God will be with us in the struggle, and He will let us know that He is. In this case, our struggle, even though it may take our prayer over, is good prayer because we are being real about ourselves and doing our best to bring God into the situation. The sins which bring about a 'dry' state are those which spring from our two instincts to survive and to reproduce. As we have seen, God does not take away these instincts so the sins which derive from them are powerful and persistent. However, in our spiritual maturing, the Holy Spirit will gradually bring them under control so that they function more in accordance with His creative purposes.

So far we have been thinking of this problem from the human point of view, when we move away from God. We must also be prepared for God Himself at times to deliberately withdraw the sense of His presence (though not, of course, His actual presence). When He so withdraws, prayer becomes largely a matter of determination and obedience. As such, these times are crucial to our growth and are probably the most important part of our prayer life, for the following reasons:

a. God is training us to pray with the highest motive. He wants us to want Him for Himself rather than for what He does for us. This will, in time, have a salutary effect upon all our motives in our life with God.
b. Because prayer then becomes a matter of obedience and determination, our wills come into play and we grow spiritually because our prayer is less dominated by softness and we learn to keep going on rather than to act according to how we feel. To reach this level demands a maturity in prayer. It means that we are learning to die to ourselves (Mark 8.34f.) and are growing in faithfulness to our Lord.
c. At these times we are shown our weakness and

emptiness. Seen positively, this is a blessing, for it drives us to God in whom alone is our life and hope. We learn that Christians live largely by God's grace rather than by any seeming ability of their own (1 Cor. 1.3ff. and 2 Cor. 12.8ff.). This shakes us out of a superficial understanding of the faith, and what a blessing that is! Until we come to some such experience of our weakness and emptiness we shall not understand our Lord's words, 'Without me you can do nothing.' When we do realise our true condition, we remember gladly and thankfully that Christ lives within us.

Emotional difficulties

Problems concerning our Lord's presence during prayer may also be due to our emotional make-up. If relationships with people are difficult for us, it will probably be that we will also find our relationship with God difficult. We are the same person no matter to whom we relate. Similarly, an emotion such as anger which has come from early experience, will mean anger towards God. He is, after all, responsible for what He has created! A critical or untrusting nature will make us critical and untrusting towards God. We may refuse to admit such things because they horrify us but that does not mean that they vanish away.

So, healing of early or later emotional injury is needed. In the prayer described in Chapter 4 the healing of God can be received into our inner life. There may also be need for further ministry and help if these hurts have been intense.

Unanswered prayer

It seems that there are quite a lot of people who believe that their prayers, or some of them, are not answered by God. As a result they may lose heart over praying, and also their faith undermined. It would appear that this problem is mostly felt when prayer is primarily that of intercession. Those whose prayer centres on a love relationship with our Lord believe that their prayer is always answered in the best way—they receive God Himself and from that relationship everything else unfolds as God works in their life.

To say this is not to denigrate intercessory prayer, but it is as well to point out that it has its problems. A major problem is that prayer may be considered as merely a means of getting from God what we think is right for ourselves or for others. If so, we may find ourselves asking for what God may not or will not do. So, if there seems to be no answer from God we should examine what we are asking and why.

It cannot be over-emphasised that God is neither unaware of our prayer nor uninvolved in it. As Christians we believe that God will live within us. Hence every thought is open to Him and there can be nothing in our lives or anybody else's life of which He is unaware. The problem must therefore be with ourselves.

Since our lives are thus open to God it follows that He will respond to any prayer we offer, even if it be totally selfish or wide of His will. We repeat the basic tenet of our faith—God is love itself. As such He cannot but respond. Therefore any seeming inaction by God should lead us to look at ourselves. We should consider what may be the cause of the apparent lack of response—for what it really means is that God is not doing what we ask. Would an affirmative answer indulge a sin, for example, or excuse us from facing life or its problems? God will not hesitate to lead us along a hard road if He knows that to be right for us. Or we may question whether our prayer is the wrong prayer in the situation, or consider that God may have something better for us.

This means that we should use any seeming unanswered prayer to learn from God. Through it He may be able to show us something of ourselves, our motives or our understanding of the faith. Rather than being disappointed with God, we may then see how He has acted and so learn of His ways. Similarly, as we attend to God in our perplexity, He may lead us to change or modify our prayer. If a sense of peace comes as a result of change, it would indicate that we are in tune with Him.

Finally, it is well to point out that much prayer *is* answered in ways we do not even notice. Because the answer has come and we have therefore ceased to worry, we may even have forgotten that we made the request, and for that reason have not thanked God for His goodness. So it is salutary to train ourselves to notice God's responses and to thank Him for each answer that we recognise. As a result we may well be surprised at how many small requests (such as for a safe road journey) have been answered. This will restore the balance in our complaints and give us more faith.

9

Praying in groups

So far we have been thinking of prayer primarily as a personal matter between God and the individual. But we are also members of the Church and so should be fully involved in prayer with others in whatever ways are open to us. A merely individual piety can be spiritually dangerous.

Through the charismatic renewal and other influences within the Church we have seen a flowering of group activity in the last two or three decades. Groups of varying kinds have become a feature of church life and have been a strength and encouragement to a large number of Christians who through them have found spiritual growth and fellowship. God has also used these groups to enrich and develop the fellowship and ministry of the church from which they sprang. The comments which follow will, it is hoped, be a help to groups of all kinds, not just those which are charismatic.

We are primarily concerned here with the prayer life of a group although general aspects of group life must, of necessity, be touched upon. Members of prayer groups should have as their primary object the desire to mature in prayer and to share in the action of God which proceeds from the prayer. That may sound obvious but it is not uncommon for people to join groups for other motives and that is bound to have an adverse effect upon the group. When members are determined to find God together and to be used by Him, the group has an atmosphere of adventure and expectancy.

The prayer we bring

The quality of the group prayer will depend upon that of the individual members. What members bring to the group will determine the nature of the prayer of the group as a whole. The primary consideration of each member should therefore be to have a personal prayer life in which God is at the centre. Each member should be seeking to know Him and be practised at allowing Him to work within and through them for His own great purposes. It cannot be said too often that it is the godward side of prayer that matters most. Therefore members should come to the group with the desire that God be honoured and worshipped and allowed to control their time together.

Such prayer has to be learned, for it seems that our natural way of operation is to see prayer as a primarily human activity. What has been said already of personal prayer is therefore important and to develop prayer along the lines described in Chapter 4 will make it possible for God to be the focus of attention and prayer when people meet together.

Waiting on God

If the Holy Spirit is to brood upon and guide the prayer, then time must be given at the outset for the group to become aware of Him. It is essential that the group learn to wait upon God. They may start with some singing and reading of the Scriptures to help bring about the right atmosphere and direct the affections towards God, but then the group should move into waiting upon God. Their aim should be to become aware of God among them. So it is important that in silence they become sensitive to Him. Silence may be difficult initially and perseverance will be required until the time comes when the group rests within it naturally. Until then there will be a tendency to feel uncomfortable and members of the group will be tempted to jump in with choruses or prayers. Once this sense of unease has been overcome, however, the group is free to be in the hands of God and there to be content, waiting upon Him as He moves upon and among them.

This initial period of waiting upon God should not be hurried, for it will set the tone of the whole meeting. This is particularly important if the group is to move from a 'sandwich' type of programme which varies little each time, to a meeting in which the Holy Spirit is allowed freedom. Such a change will call for patience because for most of us it is a new experience to move under the hand of the Spirit. Groups whose members have known renewal in the Spirit will have an advantage here.

This opening period of prayer, then, will when first practised be a learning process. Members should all have the one aim of concentrating upon God for Himself and must direct their attention and love on to Him, in as relaxed a state as possible. They will thus open themselves to God and should expect Him to be active among them. Members of the group are then able, as they look to God and worship Him in their hearts, to learn to be sensitive to Him in order to receive from Him should He wish to give to the worship. He will, of course, by His very presence, but if He gives a word, a text, a gift, it should be offered to the group to ponder upon. No doubt mistakes will be made, but unless members step out in faith they will not learn to recognise God's activity. In any case, He is quite used to seeing us make mistakes.

Worship under the Spirit of God differs from prayer that springs from human effort and activity in that the Spirit carries a group along in such a way that prayer, singing and the contribution of Scripture have a unity which is satisfying. Somehow, God makes it all one. Otherwise the worship part can become a series of unrelated words and music and the Scriptures just another unconnected part. When the Holy Spirit brings about this unity of worship, intercession and Bible study, the group know they have been with Him and the contribution of individual members has been enhanced. Experience shows that prayer groups composed of people who consider themselves very ordinary Christians can become groups strong in prayer power.

Lack of hurry should be a principle governing the whole time together. This applies as much to the intercession of a group as to that of an individual. Praying quickly through a long list results in superficial, 'automatic' prayer. But praying for a few people, with the group's full attention and with plenty of time, means that they can learn to hear what God might be saying, so He can guide the prayer. This is much more satisfying to the group and gives them more confidence as they pray.

Groups which are not in the habit of waiting upon God are therefore encouraged to do so. To receive from God in prayer can be a new idea to many people but this should not deter them from practising it. If they will stay quietly together with their attention on God and simply 'be' with Him, they will become aware that they are under His hand. He is interested. He wants to share in their prayer. It may help to offer words of adoration to keep in the right attitude of heart, or someone may slowly read out a psalm of worship or praise or other helpful scripture to create a receptive atmosphere. Once a group is accustomed to being in such prayer dependence upon God, they will not find it strange to expect God to be active. A moment's thought should convince us that Christians should regard such prayer dependence as normal. In the Bible God is a God who speaks. Relating to Him in our group worship does not mean that He will bombard us with words—we do that to Him—but that He is with us, cares and longs to serve us. He may say nothing in a session of prayer or He may say little, but we will have the right attitude, and as a result what *we* offer to Him is much more likely to please Him. Experience shows that charismatics as well as others have a lot to learn here. We all need to come before God admitting that we are a long way from arriving and that as disciples we must be forever learning.

All taking part

There are groups where the leader has an all-pervading role in praying, teaching and biblical exposition. This results in the other members being hearers only, which reduces the likelihood of personal growth. In fact, what had been a prayer time has turned into a lecture period. If the group is to function properly, each member must play his part—they all need each other. Each contribution enriches the prayer of the group while at the same time making for growth in each member. In Paul's words, 'When you come together, each one has a hymn, a lesson, a revelation, a tongue, or an interpretation. Let all things be done for edification' (1 Cor. 14.26). This can be a problem for some people who through shyness or for some emotional reason find it difficult to make a spoken contribution. The leader has a particular responsibility to encourage the diffident. Those with this problem may be helped if they are shown that long prayers are not required. A start can be made, especially in the times of worship, by breathing short prayers such as 'We adore You, Lord', 'Bless Your name, Lord', 'Thank You, Lord, for your presence here'. When all eyes are closed in worship, shy people may not feel the pressure of people's attention, particularly if they are learning awareness of God and so have their hearts fixed upon Him.

The same observation applies when there is Bible study. People can be hesitant to join in because they feel inadequate theologically or think they don't have enough experience to speak. It may help a diffident person to gain confidence if the leader asks a question which is not difficult to answer. For example, he may ask, 'John, what do you think this verse is saying about God's love?' Then, when the contribution by John has been given, it should be taken up. 'Thank you, John. Now do we all see how important that point is which John has brought out?' Not to do this, but to treat lightly or to pass over a contribution, is an effective way of silencing a sensitive person. More will be said later about the leadership of a group. While sensitive leadership such as this is important in freeing people to make their contribution, the best encouragement comes when the members are drawn together in affection and acceptance of each other.

Relating in the group

So let us give some attention to this aspect of the group's life. Groups of any kind bring people together and so provide the opportunity for relationships to be made. We are concerned here with the normal church group which is generally quite small, from five to twelve members. In such small groups each member can be recognised as a person and the friendship, warmth and acceptance we all need can be given and received. As this grows, the bond of love essential for the work of God develops. As has been pointed out, God is love and all He does is the outworking of love. Therefore if we are to be one with Him and allow Him to work within and through us, we must also become like Him. Every prayer group should therefore realise its need to grow into the true fellowship of the Spirit who, as Paul tells us, pours the love of God into our hearts (Rom. 5.5). Belonging to a group which is growing together like this becomes an experience of immense joy, for it touches our deepest need and gives confidence and a sense of worth.

However, like everything else in our faith, it is easier to speak about than to attain. That does not mean we should not work for it. It is, in fact, an essential work since God is love. But every group is made up of people who may differ in temperament, background, education, emotional condition and spiritual perception. Members must therefore be aware of this and make the necessary allowances.

To do so eases many problems. Rather than having a defensive or judgmental attitude, it is possible to choose the way of trying to understand the character and situation of others and hence their reasons for speaking and behaving as they do. For all of us this is no mean task, but membership of a group is an excellent way of learning something of the art. As we do so, it reduces the tendency to push one's own ideas and engenders a willingness to consider those of others. By God's grace, then, the temptation to be irritated by or critical of others can give way to a patient listening, to our own great benefit. It will also help us not to jump to conclusions. We may learn to become sensitive to those who feel awkward, inadequate or shy; to become aware when someone cannot express what he feels or thinks and to make allowances for hidden hurts and griefs which affect behaviour. Groups can be a good school.

Such education is demanding for anyone and so we learn slowly and make mistakes. In the small group which understands this the learning can be a gentle process. Each person can help by doing his or her best to be their natural self, not afraid to express weaknesses, fears, problems and hurts. As one member does this, others have the confidence to follow. Maybe the leader should be the one to show others the way. As this happens, barriers drop away and acceptance grow. The role of the leader is clearly important here as delicate situations can at times occur and the group must be helped to be sensitive.

The growth of true fellowship is a rich blessing which inevitably has a good effect upon the congregation of which the group is a part. The ripples go out.

Leadership

In view of this, it is clearly important to have the right leader. Few groups can exist without a leader, certainly those of five members or more. (The leader may be a man or a woman, but for convenience' sake the pronoun 'he' will be used.) Should the leader be an ordained person, one problem can be that the lay membership will tend to put him on a level different from themselves. The result can be that too much prominence is given to him and the group meeting can become dominated by him. In such a situation, it is his duty to do all he can to put himself on the same level as other members of the group. Perhaps it is preferable that leadership be invested in lay people, not only because they can be competent, but also because it is now being recognised that ministry in the Church must be more broadly based than in the past. In some churches, of course, the leadership potential is small, perhaps even nonexistent. One has sympathy with ministers of such churches, but nevertheless, the ability to delegate is one of the marks of a good leader and is apparent in those churches where there is much growth.

Some people are leaders by nature but Paul teaches us that leadership is also a gift of the Spirit (Rom. 12.8 and 1 Cor. 12.28, see GNB, NIV). Anyone called to the leadership of a group should therefore ask for the Spirit's gift. This is also specially needed where a church has a dearth of leaders.

Should there be more than one group in a local church it is advisable for the leaders to meet with the minister regularly to examine the quality of their leadership and the condition of and situation within their groups. In fact, the first group in a church should be that of the potential leaders. As they learn basic lessons and grow together they will understand how to take charge themselves. If possible, there should be both a leader and a deputy leader in each group. Apart from ensuring continuity, it means that others are being trained.

The leader's main aim is to bring the group under the hand of God so that they may grow in prayer experience and love. He should therefore be sensitive to the ethos of the group and to the situation of the individual members. This will enable him to release potentialities and recognise needs which exist. As he is able to know and assess each member, he can be in a position to anticipate danger areas. Possible animosities through character clashes, different theological attitudes and churchmanships as well as educational and social differences have all to be woven into a healthy group life. This is not done by attempting to smooth over any disagreement, but by making it possible for problems to be aired and shared in a positive and calm manner. Thus each member may widen his own understanding. This is not the easiest part of the leader's role. It is likely that he may need to give personal attention to members apart from the times of the meeting, in order to advise, clear up misunderstandings and heal hurts.

Special care may be called for with regard to new members of a group. It is often a problem to know what is best for a potential new member. He must be put into a group which is much at his own level, otherwise not only will he flounder but the other members of the group may get bored when there has to be a constant repetition of old subject matter. This may teach them patience, of course, but it can be a waste of valuable time. Should there be no other group available it means that the leader will be called upon to give additional help to the new member so that he may take his place more easily in the group. A problem can also occur when the group comes to the point where it should split. This can be a difficult time if they have grown into a true fellowship and it is hard for the two halves not to feel they have been dismembered. Pressure will then come on the leader or others in authority to let the group remain as it is. This is a mistake and such pressure should be resisted.

This last point illustrates the fact that the group exists for the larger body and not just for itself. In the church's planning and growth it is right that there should be a split in the group when it becomes too large so that others can be cared for. That has precedence over the feelings of the group members. In this relationship of the group with the larger body of the church the leader clearly has a special part. He is the appointed link from the main body and has been given authority by it. He should therefore resist any influence which would either lead to detachment or to an inward-looking attitude. The group's positive contribution to the life and work of the whole congregation should always be in the mind of the leader.

There are bound to be pressures on a leader both from his own personality and from the group. The recognition of these is half way to overcoming them. As regards himself he must be sure that he is not out to seek his own fulfilment but always acts as a servant of God and the group. He must resist the temptation to enforce his own ideas and so manipulate the members. Rather, he must give individuals and the group as a whole freedom to grow. He should also be on guard against harmful emotional reactions such as anger, impatience and jealousy. If these are under control he is able to rejoice at the growth and gifts of the members and the likelihood of his dominating the group is lessened. He should be impartial among the group members—it is natural to be drawn towards like minded and attractive people and difficult not to be influenced unduly by forceful personalities. As the leader gains experience he will be helped by constantly remembering to respect each person and to recognise their equality in God's sight.

Such considerations may cause anyone to feel too inadequate to take on the leadership of a group. In one sense this is good, for it highlights the need of the grace of God. But in our service for God we all are inadequate and when God calls us to a task He gives us the gifts we need to do it.

The group as a whole should try to see themselves as people on a pilgrimage to God, learning together as they go and rejoicing in the mutual help they give. Moving together as learners is a safe and sure way to be in the good hands of a Lord who said, 'For apart from me you can do nothing' (John 15.5).

Frequency of meeting

A word should be said about the frequency of meetings. To some degree this will depend upon the situation of the members but, generally speaking, a weekly meeting seems to be the most profitable. This is close enough in time for prayer and study to develop and facilitates growth in relationship. Also, should attendance one week be missed or a meeting be cancelled, the disruption is not a problem. If, however, the meetings are fortnightly or even less frequent, to miss one means a break of a month or more. This makes for difficulty both in individual growth and in the flow of the group life.

Should there be more than one group in the local church the groups should meet together at regular intervals to share and to affirm that they belong to the larger body. In some churches small group meetings and combined meetings alternate, in others there are combined meetings every two or three months. In this larger meeting the opportunities and problems of group life can be discussed and experiences of God can be shared, but there should also be the opportunity to mix and talk socially.

Ministry within the group

In small groups close personal relationships can develop which may lead to enough trust to permit honest sharing. Members will feel free to mention their problems and needs because the atmosphere is supportive. Inevitably this will lead to a desire to help each other and so ministry to each other can develop.

Hence as they are in prayer for one member, an inner pressure may be felt by one or more to lay on hands, either for God's special grace or for healing. It is comforting and strengthening for a person to have others ministering in this way. For those ministering it is satisfying and expresses strongly that they are standing alongside the one in need. Such ministry draws the members of the group together. They can depend upon and give to each other.

In this way the group becomes a training ground for ministry on a wider scale. In an accepting and close knit atmosphere members can feel free to learn from God and each other and so gain confidence. When, therefore, they meet a similar situation elsewhere they are able to bring what they have learnt to the new need and so step out and be used by God.

As they see that they can serve in this way, they are likely to want more training and so this may be arranged within the context of the church's overall planning. Courses can be held within the parish or people can attend courses at centres where such training is provided. In this way the church is able to serve the community more adequately.

Gifts of the Holy Spirit

In a charismatic church, the gifts of the Spirit will be manifested and learning to receive and use these gifts will be part of the training. In this personal ministry, such gifts as a word of knowledge and of wisdom, prophecy, healing, discernment, tongues and visions (or pictures in the mind) are likely to be given by the Spirit when He so desires.

It has sometimes happened in the past that someone has received a gift from God—such as the gift of healing—before receiving the baptism in the Spirit. But because of our ignorance we have denied ourselves the benefit of many other gifts that could have been used in worship and service. We may have received no teaching about the gifts in those days. Now, however, it is much more widely recognised that the Spirit is active in these ways. So it would be a pity if they were disregarded by Christians who have not received the baptism in the Spirit. This baptism certainly does facilitate the receiving of these gifts, but all Christians have the Holy Spirit and one longs for all to avail themselves of the extra help the Spirit will give as the Church faces the crying need all around.

It might, then, be helpful to say a little about the gifts. We will confine ourselves to those in 1 Corinthians 12.8–11. Paul gives others in verses 27–28 as well as in Romans 12.6–8 and Ephesians 4.11, but the latter are for more continuous ministries than gifts for a particular need. These lists, of course, do not exhaust the gifts the Spirit can have for us.

First we should describe very briefly what these gifts are. The 'words of knowledge' and 'of wisdom' refer to information that the Spirit gives which is relevant to the situation about which we are praying. This information takes us into the real need and so saves time and perplexity. 'Healing' is self-explanatory and is becoming so much part of the ministry of the Church that we need say nothing about it, except that it means that God's healing power is given for the needs of the whole person. 'Discernment' is the God-given ability to understand a situation, or the gift of insight into the personality of the one being prayed for, and the awareness of any evil presence. 'Tongues' help to make us sensitive to the Spirit Himself and so help us to receive the gift He wishes to bestow.

In worship, 'prophecy' means that God wishes to say something to those assembled. Someone will be aware of the Spirit's presence and then a word or words will come into his mind. As these are spoken out, so the Spirit will continue to give the message till it ends. Sometimes He will first cause a person to speak aloud in a tongue. If so, that same person or someone else will be given an 'interpretation' in the normal language of those present. This interpretation will not necessarily be a translation of the tongue, but will make all know the message the Spirit is giving. A 'vision' is a picture which comes into the mind, sometimes in colour. This should be described to those present. It may confirm or explain a prophecy or be a gift on its own. Should more than one person have a confirmation from the Spirit of the message given, they should say so as this authenticates the interpretation.

Paul teaches us that the Spirit alone decides whom He wishes to use for such manifestations of His working (v. 11) and so all of us should be open for such a movement by Him. Inevitably in our early experience of such things we shall feel at a loss and question what we think the Spirit is saying or doing, so it can be quite a step of faith to respond to Him. But again, mistakes are permitted. One finds that the ministry gifts come very naturally, so naturally at times that it can seem that they come only from within oneself. We all have to learn the working of the Spirit within us and we thankfully realise the importance and authenticity of these gifts when we see people blessed through them.

Prayer groups, then, can have a rich and varied life. Each must develop under the hand of God according to the potential of its members and their willingness to follow Him. Despite problems which arise, they can be a power to the church and a blessing to the members. They are worth the effort of bringing them under the hand of God, and if embraced with enthusiasm and a sense of adventure will bring their own reward.

10

The Holy Spirit and prayer (1)

All good prayer is prayer in the Holy Spirit for it is the Spirit who leads us in every way into the life of God. As Michael Ramsey has said, 'It is the Spirit who enables the Christian to pray "Abba, Father" and to acknowledge the Lordship of Jesus'. (*Be Still and Know: a Study in the Life of Prayer* (Fount, London, 1982), p. 42.) So whether we call ourselves charismatic or not, when we pray we are coming into the realm of spirit. This is not necessarily realised or experienced by many who pray and one of the invaluable consequences of the baptism in the Spirit is that this becomes abundantly clear. The world of spirit is one which no longer daunts us and neither does it entirely mystify us. Rather, even though we are only too aware of our kindergarten status, we begin to be at home in it and long to live it more fully.

That the world of spirit (of God who is Spirit and our own human spirit) should be truly our natural world, the one for which we are made, is shown us by our Lord. To the Samaritan woman He said, 'God is spirit, and those who worship him must worship in spirit and truth' (John 4.24). This means that, since God longs for us to share His life, the Holy Spirit must work to lead us into the world of pure spirit, for that is where the life of God, who is Spirit, is.

This is far removed from the materialistic world in which western society lives and which has also conditioned the lives of Christians so that the prayer of so many of us has become very materialistic. We are concerned to pray for human needs rather than to find and be with God Himself. In speaking to many who attend church one meets what amounts almost to fear when the subject of charismatic renewal is mentioned and it seems that even to think of a non-materialistic environment is more than some can manage. No doubt for them it smacks of the unknown which can be terrifying for most of us. They are afraid of the supernatural. Vague ideas of mystery, the occult and Spiritualism may be mixed together in their minds. So we can understand when some people shy away from the whole subject of charismatic renewal.

A form of religion is held which is largely human activity, a kind of religion with which people can cope. There is no questioning the sincerity of these people. Such a religious life can consist of attending worship faithfully, serving the church on committees and by various duties, giving to its work and praying, usually, in a petitionary way. Everyone knows where they are, and they mainly decide the content of their church life.

The Holy Spirit on the other hand is, as our Lord said, like the wind which 'blows where it wills, and you hear the sound of it, but you do not know whence it comes or whither it goes; so it is with every one who is born of the Spirit' (John 3.8). Once we are under the control of the Holy Spirit we have to go whichever way He takes us. So we can no longer cope, we no longer have to have control of our spiritual life. It may well be that this is the source of the fear of the supernatural. Yet our religion is fully supernatural as it both originates from and is directed to God who is totally supernatural.

As God has made us, the very heart and spring of our human nature is spirit, locked mysteriously within our being. God also is Spirit and so, if we are to become truly ourselves, we must learn to worship Him 'in spirit' as our Lord taught us. Since God is love, this must be a warm and welcoming world and one into which we should fit quite naturally. That is, in fact, what we find. While no words can describe who we meet in such prayer, our experience is one of rest, satisfaction and joy. Our own spirit recognises what we meet and, like Peter, we breathe, 'It is the Lord.' We feel enfolded and secure in our God.

What is called the baptism in the Spirit or the charismatic experience has opened up the life of spirit to many. As well as testifying to Christ the Holy Spirit Himself has become a known and loved Lord and Christ's words to the Samaritan woman that we should worship God in spirit and truth have betokened what has become a 'new and living way which he opened for us' (Heb. 10.20).

It is not then surprising that the action of our Saviour in offering to fill souls with the Holy Spirit has been so welcomed by large numbers of Christians who have been longing for more of God. This work of God has now so infiltrated the Church that it is hard to imagine that we were once ignorant of it and it has become well rooted in all major denominations and in peoples of all races and colours. It has produced fundamental changes in the vision and potentiality of life in God and in daily living. No new religion has been given but what had already been received has been illumined.

One of the major ways in which the charismatic renewal showed itself when it began in the sixties was in a desire to pray and worship God. People filled with the Spirit wanted to pray. They wanted to meet with others solely to pray. How refreshing that was! Worship lit up. It became a joy. Those of us who shared this in the early days will never want to forget the worship of the first conferences at the High Leigh conference centre at Hoddesdon. To use the word 'explosion' of worship would be wrong because it suggests an outbreak of emotionalism of which there was none. But hearts were raised in an exhilaration of worship. The sheer joy of being before God for no reason other than to worship Him was a beautiful, fulfilling and cleansing experience. We had never done anything quite like it before.

How often previously had we been dissatisfied with our worship of God. We wanted to worship Him but somehow, though we put our hearts into singing the Gloria, the Te Deum and similar acts of worship there had been something missing. Now we found our hearts raised by the Spirit to adore, love, praise and thank God. Worship flowed from us and it was a refreshing and exhilarating change from the past.

Worship and prayer had, in fact, taken on a radical change. It was not *our* worship as we had regarded it previously. Now we had our first vision of prayer and worship initiated and directed by the Spirit. Perhaps the truth is not so black and white as that, but it was a change of such significance that it felt like that.

The sense of God's presence made us realise that God was involved in our worship of Him. That may sound obvious but for so many Christians it was and still is not a joyous assumption, as participation in some worship makes evident. A lively realisation that God truly is involved and is welcoming our worship of Him makes us open to Him. This is why we can expect the Spirit to move among us with His gifts both to lift worship and to speak to us.

Such worship also makes our being together a thing of importance. This has been realised in liturgical circles and has found expression in the introduction into the Eucharist of more corporate participation. But it seems that it is in churches where the renewal has infiltrated that the Peace, for example, has been a most welcomed response to our new appreciation of being the Body of Christ and members one of another. In earlier days, how often did those of us who are clergy try to wean our congregations from the idea of 'making my Communion' by teaching the corporate nature of the sacrament? Where all our exhortation failed, the

Holy Spirit wonderfully succeeded in bringing a warmth into worship and a long overdue recognition and acceptance of one another. It means so much to *show* love and to see barriers slowly break down. Even so, it is not without sympathy that one realises that for some people such personal contact, both emotional and physical, causes problems. The Holy Spirit is the very One who is able to teach us sensitivity towards them.

No doubt in those early days we were experiencing the first flush of glorious discovery and inevitably as the years have passed this first flush has faded. But the fundamental change has stayed with us and we have continued to be under the Spirit with the same love and desire for God but expressing it in the more disciplined way that the day to day living of faith demands. Perhaps whatever 'froth' there was has gone, but at its best there never was froth. The continuance, growth and deepening of the renewal is proof of this.

Mistakes have been made, people have been hurt, there has been much to learn and re-learn and theology has lagged behind experience. This is what the early Church found too, and it is hardly surprising when you consider the profundity of the experience. Disturbance in fact points to the importance of this work of God. Anything of small significance would hardly have ruffled the waters of the mainline churches. We must pray that the best will prevail and bless the Church. Unfortunately we are very frail human beings, but our Lord heartens us by letting us know that 'with God all things are possible'.

At the present day the influence of renewal on congregations affected by it is strong. Naturally it varies from church to church, but there is no mistaking a charismatic congregation. We are told that churches accepting the renewal have the biggest growth in membership and the sharpest rise in giving. Even in many non-charismatic churches the effect is felt in such ways as the use of choruses, dance and drama.

These and other expressions of worship and teaching are, naturally, found in charismatic church worship. Perhaps the most arresting change is the sense of warmth and of belonging together. This is as it should be since the Spirit, as Paul teaches us, pours the love of God into our hearts—not that this is easy to achieve nor does it usually come without misunderstandings and hurts. This warmth is felt not only in the welcome we receive as we enter the church, but during the whole service. It is epitomised in the sharing of the Peace. This can become a happy unhurried family time.

One notices also a liveliness about the worship and a sense of expectancy. People expect God to speak to them through the hymns and choruses, the reading of the Scriptures and the sermon. The latter has taken on a new significance in churches where previously it had been a ten minute homily. Teaching is important, people want to learn, and there is, as a result, more exposition of the Bible. Also, the singing matters to the worshippers and is congregationally based rather than choir based. In addition, many churches have their own liturgical dance group and banners have come into their own.

Looking at worship as it is in renewed Anglican churches, the general pattern appears to be that the morning services keep pretty well to the service book in use. Largely this service is the Eucharist. What has been said above about the warmth of fellowship, the Peace and liveliness of worship is evident, but generally speaking the gifts of the Spirit are not in obvious use. These seem to be given in the evening when the services may be less formal. It is quite common to move from Evensong into an informal kind of worship or to have a further free-form service after Evensong. It is quite clear that we are still in the process of integrating this experience of the Spirit with the official forms of worship and this process is bound to continue for some time. We certainly do not want to lose either the Church's liturgy nor the unfolding and enrichment of it which the Spirit can give us. Perhaps innovation will help, as we are finding with the introduction of the healing ministry into services. The best solution will come, one imagines, through the maturing of prayer. That is the way the Spirit will most surely be able to lead us and we can be confident that if He is allowed to perform this welding together, all will benefit richly. We would hope that as He moves He will bring us all more to a common mind, so that the worship of the Church as a whole can become more worthy of the God who calls us to Him. New services give the opportunity to allow a measure of freedom and there seems no reason why gifts, ministry and other expressions of the Holy Spirit's presence should not be given place within liturgical services.

Music in worship

The torrent of new choruses and their popularity is clear evidence that they meet a need. While it is true that not everybody likes them and musicians can look askance at them, they are no worse than many hymns when they are orchestrated and sung by people of professional standard. Perhaps we should all remember the words that C. S. Lewis put into the mouth of Screwtape—that when Wormwood's patient attended church he would be given 'one shabby little book containing corrupt texts of a number of religious lyrics, mostly bad'. In our worship of God we should do our best to make our words and music as fine as possible, and it is encouraging that competent musicians are now helping us to combine the best of traditional and modern hymns and choruses.

Great numbers of people find that they can express their feelings through choruses better than through many hymns. Books such as *Hymns Ancient and Modern* are deficient in hymns which express personal experience of the Christian life and it requires hard work to make some of them raise the soul to worship. Nevertheless, to lose the Church's rich heritage of spirituality as enshrined in hymns would be an unforgivable deprivation. In both church worship and renewal meetings or groups, therefore, we would hope that the resources of both musical contributions would be used to glorify God.

The shortcomings of hymn books is clearly recognised by the issue of such additional publications as *A Hundred Hymns for Today* and the inclusion, in new editions of hymn books, of more hymns of worship and personal devotion and choruses, most of which are of relatively modern date.

While choruses are a true and necessary expression of worship and praise, their use is not without problems and it is worth giving some attention to their use. They must glorify God, not merely please singers or musicians, and it truly is a joy to see eyes closed and faces lit up as choruses known by heart are sung under the Spirit. But because choruses are liked and can speak strongly they are sometimes strung together one after another with no apparent connection. There may be a place for this: it is like the way people once stood round the piano on Sunday evenings singing hymns. When, however, we are in worship under the Spirit, He is the one who should direct our choice of choruses, and we should learn to allow Him to do so. One of the most moving uses of choruses is when they rise out of a group in prayer. One member is moved by the Spirit to begin and the others take it up with eyes closed and with all attention on the Lord. Since the words are known by heart, such singing does not require the turning up of books and so there is no disturbance of the worship as people sing.

However, though choruses may be the main form of music at meetings and in groups, there is no reason why they should have the monopoly. Many hymns express aspects of our faith more beautifully and deeply than some choruses in which verses follow one another in an unrelated series of thoughts.

Professional musicians are not essential in church services or at meetings, but without a certain competence, players of musical instruments can be a hindrance to worship. Therefore no group should play in church unless they have practised together sufficiently to be able to lead the praise well. Some pianists and guitarists have a wonderful gift. They seem to know all the choruses, they can take up a chorus from the meeting in the right key and they can bring just the right chorus in at the right time, fitting beautifully into the subject of prayer, Bible reading or teaching. Under their hand the music raises people to heights of prayer and praise. But those who fumble for the right note as they take up the singing of the meeting can be exasperating.

While there can be problems with music, they should serve only to move us to offer the best possible to God and to learn to use the gift of music in any style to enhance worship and to raise our souls to the throne of grace. In this, singing in tongues can be a rich blessing. One is aware of the Spirit as He blends our voices into one harmonious sound and lifts us up in sheer praise. It is just as moving when He brings all to a close together and there follows a time of rich and beautiful silence.

11

The Holy Spirit and prayer (2)

The gifts of the Spirit in worship

Within the renewal it is probable that the gifts of the Spirits are most evident in the healing and counselling ministries. No doubt this is because there is such an obvious need for them. One is confronted not only with suffering which calls out a longing for its alleviation but also with situations where the light and guidance of the Holy Spirit alone can discern and direct. So gifts such as the words of knowledge and wisdom, healing, discernment and the granting of visions are invaluable.

In these situations we are driven to God for His leading and action. This means that the development of a good prayer relationship with God is essential for this makes possible a growing sensitivity to the Holy Spirit. Though the need seems more obvious when we are confronted with distress, it is no less essential to be in close touch with God with regard to the worship gifts. These gifts, as already stated, are usually prophecy, tongues and interpretation, visions, and discernment. It is the quality of our prayer which makes us open and alive to God and able to respond to Him when He wishes to move through us. This need for growing maturity in prayer cannot be over-emphasised. When God is real to us through prayer and we are accustomed to allowing Him to move within us, then the gifts will come as God desires for we have given Him the ground on which to work. Where such a prayer relationship does not exist, people will feel inadequate to judge whether it is truly the Spirit who is motivating them, and therefore fearful of stepping out under Him. Contrariwise, should a person be someone without inhibitions, the likelihood is that what he does will not be of God. This is clearly expressed in 2 Peter, 'For prophecy never had its origin in the will of man, but men spoke from God as they were carried along by the Holy Spirit' (1.21, NIV). While anyone would hesitate to put himself on the level of the Old Testament prophets, the principle is plain enough.

Further, if we are to allow the Spirit to speak, then there must in worship be a quiet and orderly waiting upon Him. Too much noise by praying aloud and singing disrupts attention. The minister in church or the leader of a group or meeting should therefore see to it that these do not dominate. He should also encourage silence so that people stop feeling awkward when it descends upon them. Of course, there are times in worship when all are lifted to adoration and praise. This is thrilling because it is the consequence of the movement of the Spirit. It is, however, clear from 1 Corinthians 13 and 14 that Paul was very aware of this need for a quiet and orderly waiting upon God, for this is the theme of those two chapters.

For the Spirit to use us, it is not sufficient that the atmosphere of the worship be conducive. We each receive and respond to His touch when we are in a state of inner quietness. Then we can direct our loving attention on to the Spirit who is within and so can be in a position of expectancy, ready should He wish to speak. If the people present are in this attentive relationship with God, then the tone of the meeting as a whole will be right.

When we first experience the fullness of the Spirit, the sense of His presence can be so strong that we easily and joyously respond as He manifests His gifts through us. Gifts can come to us in these early days because the activity of the Spirit is sovereign. It is not, therefore, necessarily a sign of maturity if a gift is received. It is no less a true work of God for that, and is to be accepted with thankfulness. As time goes on the first flush of delight naturally fades. Then it is replaced by the need for a disciplined attention to Him. This is a more mature condition than the earlier one and so should not cause questioning or self-criticism.

Some people have found that the anointing of the Spirit has come with a lighter touch as they have grown under His hand. This makes us wait more attentively upon Him, and at times our obedience to what we believe He is asking of us calls for greater faith. But when we obey, we realise that what we have done in response to the Spirit has His hallmark upon it. Perhaps this is one way the Spirit can teach us faith. It is one of the joys of being in His hands that constantly He is active in teaching us. So we can learn to be alert. Life with Him is never dull.

Some have also found that at certain periods the Spirit has manifested a gift and then it has virtually ceased for a time. There is biblical precedent for this in the case of healings, through Peter (Acts 5.15–16) and Paul (Acts 19.11).

It should be strongly emphasised that the gifts must be under healthy control. As has already been pointed out, any message from God should be first examined and pondered and then acted upon. No genuine person will object to a message, apparently from the Spirit, being tested: if he does, then his very objection must give cause for suspicion.

So Paul wisely lays it down that two or three at the most may give words from God and the others should weigh what is said (1 Cor. 14.17–33). Some groups exult in a plethora of prophecies, tongues and visions to such an extent that by the end one is left with an undigested mass of words. The result is that nothing has really taken root in people's hearts and no one has been edified. In such circumstances one can be sure that much of what has purported to be from the Spirit has a human origin. This cannot honour God.

Careful prayer, thought and study of words given at meetings is particularly necessary if the words relate to such important matters as the future ministry of the church or directions for its growth. In such cases, no action on a prophecy should be taken until the leaders have thoroughly examined it and themselves have received confirmation from God that this is His word to them. This caution should not make the church hesitate to ask the Lord for guidance. He alone knows precisely the condition of the congregation and the neighbourhood which they serve. If God gives direction, the plans will prosper. It would therefore seem sensible for the church to learn the way God is leading them. They should be prepared to wait patiently for the Lord's leading to be revealed. This may take some months.

Should a church therefore decide to wait upon God for His guidance there will need to be a disciplined listening. Whether a few people are chosen for this task or whether it is decided to have an open meeting, it is a wise rule that any speaking or praying, apart from silent waiting upon God, should be confined to intimations thought to be from Him. As these come they can be examined and prayed over, and if accepted as from God, will be the stepping stone to the next communication from Him. So the regular waiting upon God can continue until it is believed that the mind of God has been revealed. When a small group has been entrusted with this, they should then bring what they have received to the Parochial Church Council or other authority. If the PCC confirm that the guidance is from God, then action can be taken by the church.

Again, it should be emphasised that since God is love and the Holy Spirit 'pours the love of God into our hearts', this fruit of the Spirit is the source and end of all that God does. The gifts therefore are the outworking of God's love. When they are genuinely from the Spirit, this is clearly evident and all are blessed.

The gift of tongues

In the early days of the renewal, praying in tongues (or 'in the Spirit') was a cause of much controversy and even denigration. Looking back now one wonders why there should have been such a strong reaction, particularly as it has such clear biblical endorsement in 1 Corinthians and the Acts of the Apostles. Be that as it may, to those who have used it well, it has proved a valuable gift of God from which the whole Church benefits. We believe that when we pray in tongues the Holy Spirit Himself is praying within us and the manner in which He moves the throat muscles and the tongue to form a language is a constant source of awe. It is essential that we do not know the meaning of the sounds that come, for otherwise they would so easily be thought of as of our own making. Since it is the Holy Spirit's prayer, we have confidence and can relax into it, knowing that He prays according to the will of God.

In describing it, Sister Rosslyn of the Community of St Andrew once said, 'It affords a real release of the Spirit in the areas of our subconscious and perhaps unconscious, and for this reason is a threshold experience as we learn to yield ourselves into the hands of God.' So it is the experience of many that regular daily prayer in the Spirit, aloud or silent, has a formative effect upon the personality as the Spirit works not only within the fears, the dark places and hurts of our hidden inner life, but also encourages the growth of the best of our personality. This action of the Spirit builds us up in confidence in God and in ourselves through cleansing and healing. When we pray silently in the Spirit, He makes His prayer and as we are aware of the language going on within, we share in it in spirit and heart.

This gift means that throughout the day we can be in the prayer of the Spirit of God. Praying in tongues is a great aid to recollection as it helps to lead us to live constantly in the presence of God, for when we pray in tongues the Spirit directs our attention and heart towards God and we are aware that we are one with Him. This form of prayer has a rich effect upon our own prayer in other ways. We all have times when it is difficult to pray. Sometimes we simply do not feel like praying. Then, if we pray in tongues, we are quickly lifted into an awareness of God and a desire for Him. At other times we can be plagued with feelings of different kinds—we can feel depressed, disheartened, disappointed, hurt or misunderstood. When we pray in tongues at such moments we find to our joy that the Spirit does not suffer from these things and He raises our prayer above them as we are brought in touch with God.

This gift means so much also when we are bewildered in a situation and do not know how to pray. Then we rest in the Spirit and allow Him to pray through us, while we offer our prayer to Him knowing that His will be the perfect prayer and He will take our prayer into His.

As there is nothing ecstatic in this gift nor any

losing of conscious control, we are taken into the tranquillity of the Spirit within us. As we use this way of prayer during the day so we tend to be kept in this tranquillity. It is always available to us but we have the privilege of starting or ending it as we feel the need. During the night also, when sleep does not come because of a racing mind, anxiety or problems, many have found that to pray in the Spirit can lead to a quietening of the thoughts and have even found that their own spirits can be raised into praise.

This then is a precious gift of God which can have a gently pervasive action upon us. Those who have received it are urged to use it each day for a period of ten minutes or more and others are encouraged to seek it.

The charismatic prayer meeting

The growth of charismatic prayer groups has been a boon to Christians who have been enriched by the Spirit and have felt inhibited in a larger congregation. So the charismatic prayer meeting has become an adjunct to the Sunday worship with more freedom both because everyone is like-minded and also because of the smaller numbers. The large meetings also satisfy a need, but here we are mainly concerned with the smaller type.

While there is no doubt that these group meetings are a boon both to the church and the group members there is still much to be learnt about being led by the Spirit. There is commonly a tendency to keep to a fairly regular pattern, which can be a human arrangement with the worship including too large a proportion of chorus singing and intercessory prayer.

If these groups are to become more Spirit led, what has been offered in Chapter 9 may help. Any group which is to grow in awareness of and leading by the Holy Spirit must give time to wait upon Him and this will include learning to feel at home in the silence. Though not essential, it can assist the members if they form a close circle and hold hands while waiting upon God. This helps to give a sense of oneness which enables members to be more sensitive to the Spirit and eases any sense of isolation in the silence. So together they can fix their hearts upon God and when this is done regularly the group develops the habit of listening as a body to the Spirit. This will call for perseverance in some groups but the result will be well worth the effort. Once this ability to wait upon the Spirit is learnt, it will influence the whole meeting.

It will mean that people will learn to surrender themselves to the Spirit, realising that He will move among them. They can then be freed from the necessity to adhere to a fixed pattern. At one group where over the years they learnt to be led by the Spirit, they knew at each meeting that He had spoken to them. At times it was teaching, at another they were given encouragement. When necessary they received direction in their problems. At some meetings burdens were put on their hearts and they even received gentle rebuke when that was necessary. The form of their time together was never the same two weeks running. So they came together anticipating this and eager to see what the Spirit would do.

When a group develops in this way, its members will be led to look beyond themselves because they will realise without any doubt that God is in control. As they see His activity in their small group the realisation will come of what He can do on a larger scale. So the life and witness of their church can come to be seen from the standpoint of God's activity. This sends them back to God in prayer because they soon appreciate the need to be at one with Him as He moves among and through them. So they can move full circle: learning to pray to release the Spirit leads to His action which in turn sends them back to Him as they co-operate in the working through of it.

Learning to be under the Spirit in this manner does not obviate the need of good leadership. On the contrary, it enhances the need, for there is much to learn and a mature and experienced person will keep a light but firm control. He will recognise when someone is not acting under the Spirit and he will help the members of the group to understand how the Spirit is leading them and to see the significance of what He says and does.

A vision of life under the Holy Spirit is presented to us in an impressive prayer by Bishop Carey, at one time bishop of Bloemfontein. It is the prayer one would love to see fulfilled in one's own life and so is a fitting conclusion to this chapter.

O Holy Spirit of God—
    Come into my heart and fill me:

I open the windows of my soul to let Thee in.
I surrender my whole life to Thee:
Come and possess me, fill me with light and
truth.
I offer to Thee the only thing I really possess,
My capacity for being filled by Thee.
Of myself I am an unprofitable servant,
An empty vessel.
Fill me so that I may live the life of the Spirit.
The life of Truth and Goodness: the life of
Beauty and Love,
The life of Wisdom and Strength.
And guide me today in all things:
Guide me to the people I should meet or help:
To the circumstances in which I can best serve
God,
Whether by my action or by my sufferings.
But, above all, make Christ to be formed in me,
That I may dethrone self in my heart
And make Him King.
Bind and cement me to Christ by all Thy ways
Known and unknown:
By holy thoughts, and unseen graces,
And sacramental ties:
So that He is in me, and I in Him,
Today, and for ever.

12

Contemplative prayer

In Chapter 4 a method of prayer was described by which we can learn to relax and come into the presence of God. This 'being with God' or 'looking at God' with our loving attention is to move towards the form of prayer which is called contemplation. If it is God's will that a soul be raised to contemplation, perseverance in that method can lead naturally into it. It is probably true that contemplative prayer has in the past been considered to be for great mystics and not for the ordinary run of Christians. Fortunately this view is fading. We may not ascend to the mystical heights of the great ones, but we certainly can enter into this kind of prayer. Increasing numbers of people nowadays are, in fact, having a desire for contemplative prayer. They find that the form of prayer taught, or not taught, in the past is unsatisfying. Something inside them wants to pray to find God Himself.

There is a delightful story of an incident in the life of the curé of Ars in France. He used to notice that an old man had the habit of coming into church each day about midday, sitting there for quite a long time seemingly doing nothing and then departing. One day the curé asked the old man, 'Father, what do you do when you come into church each day?'

The old man replied, 'I sit and look at Jesus and Jesus looks at me.'

That is a description of contemplative prayer and it was spoken by a nineteenth-century French peasant. The Holy Spirit can direct anyone for whom contemplation is right, to desire to contemplate God. Not all people by any means find their hearts drawn to pray in this way and it is not for us to judge whether one form of prayer is higher than another. The better prayer is always the one which is content only to be in a state of oneness with God, but this is possible through other types of prayer also and we must each go the way the Spirit and our own temperament lead. Because there is clearly a need for some teaching about contemplative prayer an attempt is here made to say something helpful.

St Teresa of Avila uses the analogy of watering a garden to describe the journey in prayer of those led into contemplation. This journey is from the kind of prayer which is mainly our own activity to that where God is the prime mover. She says there are different ways in which a garden may be watered. One way is when we do the watering by drawing water from a well. That is a very laborious business. A less laborious way is by the use of a water-wheel with a windlass. If there is a stream or spring in the garden our work is cut down. The best way of all is when the Lord waters the garden Himself by sending heavy rain and there is then no labour on our part at all. Her main point is that as we progress in prayer it becomes increasingly a God-activated relationship, till with contemplative prayer as our part, we just gaze upon God leaving Him 'to send the rain'.

We begin to want to contemplate God when the desire is given us by the Spirit. A longing comes for God Himself, and we go to God with no requests or problems for solution but solely to find Him. Something inside us is crying out for God Himself. We know instinctively that this will not be through words. We sense that silence is where we will find Him. So when we come to pray we concentrate our attention and our will upon seeking God. This is possible because God in His love and mercy gives Himself to the soul which desires to have Him and so He is there within us. It is there that we seek Him.

At first it is with heart and mind that we meet God but as we continue in our seeking we become aware that our spirit also is involved; within us our spirit is contemplating God who is Spirit. But also it dawns upon us that the Spirit of God is looking at us. It is Spirit to spirit. This situation may go on for some time before we are aware of what is actually happening. At first we will have the realisation that in some way God and we are at one. As it is Spirit to spirit, our emotions are not usually involved (unless God desires to touch them). We are not aware of our feelings, but simply of the spirit-relationship. We are with God, resting in Him and longing for Him to reveal Himself—which He does in His own indescribable way. As the peasant said, 'Jesus looks at me.'

This meeting with God in spirit is a new experience for us. As Paul wrote, 'Even if we did once know Christ in the flesh, that is not how we know him now' (2 Cor. 5.16, JB). We do not meet flesh. We meet what seems 'Nothing'—No Thing—for God in His spiritual nature is not like anything to be found in the created universe. But though we cannot comprehend the ineffable God, we know He is there. It is as though we are looking directly at the sun and failing to see it. Hence such approaches to God have been described in phrases like 'the cloud of unknowing' or 'the dazzling darkness'. Nevertheless there is the awareness that such prayer is an encounter with a Person and the experience is one of being wanted and loved and kept safe.

Perhaps it should be said at this point that the desire for God can be strong even in the early stages of this way of prayer. As a result we may not be content to rest in God but may strain for Him. To do so can lead to prayer becoming impossible because our spirit has become 'knotted'. Evelyn Underhill has pointed out to us that we can strain our spirit muscles just as we can strain our physical ones and we lose the use of the former as much as we do the latter. We then have no alternative but to cease to pray and allow our spirit to relax. We learn through this quite forcibly that our part in prayer is to let God do the work. We do not bring about God's will by striving but by listening and obeying. So, as we learn to contemplate God we become more willing to put ourselves into His hands and wait with patience upon Him. This does not mean that action is obviated. Good prayer leads to our carrying out the will of God as we see it and so service in one form or another will derive from our prayer.

All of us who pray like to feel the presence of God. It is a comfort, joy and encouragement. When we enter the way of contemplative prayer the time comes when God leads us to realise that we have to be weaned from wanting what we like to desiring what He wants. This is a full turn round for some of us. As we desire what God wants we can set out under Him to enter into His life by learning to be at one with His will for us as we walk the path of prayer He desires for us. This is a demanding discipline but if God is calling us to this way of prayer, we will follow Him. We know that many of those who have trod this way before us warn us not to seek 'consolations'. We are not in prayer primarily for our own wishes but for God Himself.

This does not mean that such prayer has no joy in it. Quite the contrary. To be with God is our joy. But it does mean that we accept whatever God does as the best possible thing for us at that moment, and the most that we are in a position to receive from Him. This saves us from false imaginings of what to expect from God and helps us to rest contentedly in Him.

Other things follow from this. The first is that only the grace of God is sufficient for such a turn round. This grace must lead us along a road of humility and awareness of our own lamentable condition, with the resultant understanding of our need to trust Him and so allow Him to have control of us. It also helps us not to test our growth in prayer by the sense of pleasure we get from it. In any case, we are the last people to make an assessment of our own spiritual condition. A better test is the measure of our obedience to God. When God does touch us in prayer it is wise not to broadcast such moments. They are given not for our pride but for God's particular purpose (which we should try to understand) or as a sheer expression of His delight in us.

As a result, in the 'dry' periods we are less tempted to allow prayer to slip. Although it is certainly not so easy to pray when God takes away the sense of His presence, the desire for Him which the Spirit has implanted will keep us seeking Him. Our little bit of love for God will also help us at these times. But, as Brother Roger of Taizé has told us, we are not out for ease but to find and have God. He writes, 'Prayer, descending into the depths of God, is not there to make life easy for us. Pray: not for any kind of result, but in order to create with Christ a communion in which we are free' (*Struggle and Contemplation* (Mowbray, Oxford, 1983), p. 103). But prayer should lead us to the understanding that God wills the best for us and so there is a sense of adventure as we are led into the heart of God.

Freedom and adventure are both part of our experience as we travel the contemplative road. This freedom is not only the ability to be truly ourselves in God's presence but also the sense that we are moving out of the restrictive realm of flesh and blood into the unrestricted realm of spirit. All Christians do, of course, live in two worlds at the same time but in contemplative prayer we roam into the higher reaches of the spiritual world. In Paul's words, '. . . we look not to the things that are seen but to the things that are unseen; for the things that are seen are transient, but the things that are unseen are eternal' (2 Cor. 4.18). As we pray our spirit is learning to sense the unseen 'atmosphere' and so is becoming free to express itself and be nourished.

What Paul calls the 'eternal weight of glory' is the source of the adventure also. Moving into the world of spirit is moving into the very life of God Himself which is unimaginably rich and unfathomable to our tiny finite understanding. We will never do more than wonder at the vastness of glory. But in prayer we know that this is our true home and that for eternity we will increasingly savour it. So we have this sense of adventure, of embarking upon the greatest adventure offered to humanity. Our experience of it may be tiny; we may seem at times to make little progress; during the dry periods we may feel only too earthbound, but once we have the 'taste' for it we will keep on going on. This 'keeping on going on' is one of the hallmarks of contemplative praying. It is essential because there are no quick results in this prayer. We are used to an 'instant' world, but God's action takes place in the context of eternity.

Because the Spirit creates a longing for God, there inevitably grows a desire to be rid of the things that hinder this. The obvious thing is sin. The need to be cleansed can grow very strong because within the realm of the Spirit and in the presence of God sin stands silhouetted. Because God is love this has never the character of condemnation, but we come to hate what both separates us from God and grieves Him. So we long to be holy, both to be one with God and to be like Him. We have moved out of the negative level of feeling convicted of sin into the positive level of longing to be pure in heart. As our Lord said, 'Blessed are the pure in heart, for they shall see God' (Matt. 5.8). This was the cry of the Dutch mystic Jan van Ruysbroeck, who said, 'If anyone should ask me what I would most desire, I would say, "Lord, give me a pure heart."' The desire to see God urges us on to battle against sin and to be made pure in heart.

Inevitably this way of prayer leads us into silence. There is no sound with spirit. The language is not the language of words but of being. We are being with God. We are being with God and are open to the influence of God beaming upon our spirit. So we remain still in body, mind and spirit looking to Him and wanting to become aware of what is flowing from Him. It is a form of listening, though not to sound. We may at times receive thoughts, ideas and understandings, but generally it will be a steady contemplation with no 'message' from Him. It seems that the majority of time so spent consists of a hidden action of God while we wait upon Him in the silence.

This silence becomes a constant and loved atmosphere of inner life. It is a warm, welcoming environment which is a sturdy security and contains nothing which can destroy our unity with God. So we come to love it because it leads us to God and because it is of God. Through it we touch a God who is imperturbable and unmoved in His essence no matter how much this discordant world tears itself to pieces with hate and fear. God remains unchanged in love and with Him in the silence we meet His tranquillity.

So this prayer of resting in God touches our inmost need. We are happy to be quiet and leave Him free to do His work in us. It is 'looking unto Jesus' and in so doing we are preparing ourselves in the best way possible for life when we leave this world. No words can describe what that life will be, but maybe the lines of F. W. Faber are not too wide of the mark:

> Father of Jesus, love's reward,
> What rapture will it be,
> Prostrate before thy throne to lie,
> And gaze and gaze on thee!

Some great souls have been granted flashes of that rapture, and they have been those who have risen to the heights of contemplation of God. Ordinary mortals which most of us are can at least walk along the same road even though we may not get so far.

Both praying in the Spirit and the Jesus Prayer can not only keep us in an awareness of God but also lead us into contemplative prayer. Some attention has already been given to praying in the Spirit and we have said that as we develop its use it brings us into a consciousness of God. It should be mentioned that some persistence and practice is required to reach this point. People vary as they begin to pray in the Spirit. With some it starts with just a few words and requires determination to continue until the flow of sound comes. Others have immediately a rich flow of language. However it may be given, practice is necessary to reach the place where through it we have a constant means of worship and awareness of God at our disposal.

The Jesus Prayer, which we have from the Orthodox Church, is a form of repetitive prayer. The full prayer is, 'Lord Jesus, Son of God, have mercy on me a sinner.' By the repetition of these words, or shorter forms of them, the prayer can move from the mind to the heart and can there continue almost of its own accord, uniting us with God. The Archimandrite Sophrony in his book *His life is mine* describes five stages of this deepening process: verbal, mental, centred on the heart, self-propelling, and a gentle flame of love in the heart (p. 113). Metropolitan Anthony in his book *Living Prayer* speaks more generally and describes the effect of the prayer in these words, 'More than any other prayer, the Jesus Prayer aims at bringing us to stand in God's presence with no other thought but the miracle of our standing there and God with us, because in the use of the Jesus Prayer there is nothing and no one except God and us' (p. 88).

Those who use it regularly find that these words are true and so we value the prayer. As with praying in the Spirit, the Jesus Prayer naturally requires development until that also flows naturally. Both have the advantage that they can be used at almost any time such as when walking, travelling, during a waiting period, as well as in illness or disturbing situations when it is not possible to settle down to sustained prayer. The use of these two forms of prayer are also a boon during the dry periods of prayer or when concentration is difficult. They help us to hold our attention and affection on to God and so are a comfort.

The contemplative writers

Those who are led into this way of prayer may like to be made aware of the contemplative writings. There is a rich treasury of writings by men and women who have gone farthest into contemplative prayer. They represent a wide variety of nationality and personality from both the Eastern and Western Churches, though for most of us it is the writings of the western tradition which are best known. As truth and beauty are mediated through very different composers in works of music, so these writings come through each personality in a way distinctive of the channel God has used and so we should each find the ones which most readily speak to us.

In reading them they kindle our desire for God because their writings breathe both His presence and the atmosphere of prayer, and they speak of experience of God in prayer for which we ourselves long. There is, with most of them, an attractive winsomeness and a simplicity and directness which is the mark of people who are masters of their subject. Each, in his or her own way, set before us how to contemplate God; they describe their own experience of Him; they show us how to keep close to God, and how the power of sin and the domination of the world can be broken.

For them all, love for God is the consuming passion of their lives. For this they have been willing to forgo everything else and so the road has often been a hard one. But they have by God's grace persevered until they have reached what is called the state of union with Him. What they write, therefore, is living experience of God through prayer and they have given us a wealth of example and teaching through what they have learnt on the way.

We should therefore take advantage of their own works and also read the stories of their lives. Some are now published as paperbacks. In addition there are very many books by those who have studied their works and these help to enlighten us and explain concepts or language with which we are unfamiliar.

It should also be pointed out that in addition to this legacy from past centuries there also exist the writings of those who have travelled this path in the present century, and from these also we may benefit.

Copies of these books can be found in public libraries but the most comprehensive collections are in retreat houses and in religious houses. Those of us who make retreats will have the opportunity of exploring such collections. At this point it might be right to encourage the habit of making a regular retreat. There everything is done to assist us to spend time being close to God and to explore the realm of silence. Such time well used can bring much benefit to the quality of our daily prayer relationship with our Lord.

In the Appendix some suggestions for further reading are given.

13

Public worship

As Christians we believe that worship is our highest activity and as such it has to be learnt. The centre of worship is our devotion to God and this flows into prayer which is the expression of our devotion. So we have to be taught how to come to God, how to live at one with Him and how devotion to Him can grow. As members of congregations are in such a relationship with God, worship will inevitably ensue.

The privilege of worship

We are urged in the letter to the Hebrews not to neglect our coming together and this is said with good reason, for public worship is an essential part of our Christian life and in particular it is a healthy and necessary balance to our personal prayer. Since our destiny is to adore for ever the glory of God, we should take every present opportunity to allow the Holy Spirit to lead us into that experience of it which is possible to us in the world.

The Bible at times gives us tantalising hints of what worship can be. One of these is the incident that happened to Jacob when on his way to Haran. In a dream he saw a ladder reaching from earth to heaven. Angels were ascending and descending on it and the Lord of heaven above it communicated with Jacob. This dream had a profound effect upon Jacob, for when he woke he had come to a new awareness of God, 'Surely the Lord is in this place; and I did not know it. . . . How awesome is this place! This is none other than the house of God, and this is the gate of heaven' (Gen. 28.16–17).

It would seem that it is just this of which we also should become aware. The ladder indicates that earth and heaven are one in a deeper unity than most of us imagine. Not only are we in the presence of angels and 'surrounded by a great cloud of witnesses' of those who have gone before us from this world but if we belong to God we are already in heaven. Heaven is God, and God has given Himself to live within us if we have so desired. Put another way—we live, as Jesus taught us, in the kingdom of heaven. Christians 'are not of the world', said Jesus, 'even as I am not of the world' (John 17.16). We live in two worlds at the same time, this world and the kingdom of heaven. In Paul's words, we 'sit in the heavenly places in Christ Jesus' (Eph. 2.6). We should be learning what it means to be in such a state of grace. The earth is linked to heaven.

As such, the earth is full of the glory of God. God pervades His universe and never are we out of His presence. Our worship of Him should mean a growing awareness of this glorious fact. Our own worship is one with the angels as well as with those who, with them, glory in the greater light of the presence of God. As we learn to look at the things that are unseen and eternal, we can become sensitive both to the presence of God 'in whom we live and move and have our being' (Acts 17.28) and to the vast throng who see God on the other side of death. While many of us believe we should not try to get in touch with those who have passed on, it helps to send our love to certain of them through Christ. So we can ask Him to give our love to dear ones and to others with whom we have shared suffering in this world. In so doing, we can know that we are one with them in our Lord. The perfect setting for this is within the Eucharist. We should do this not for any selfish reason but that we may join with them in the worship of God. We are one family in His love.

When we come to church, then, it is to learn to have our eyes on God. We should not come with our eyes on ourselves to get 'my bit of help', though by God's grace we may get it. We certainly will gain if we truly put our hearts into adoring and loving God. True worship is an unselfish act. In it we acknowledge God as Lord and we make the true response of creatures who have come from Him and on whom we depend for life. Because God is love, this is a joy, not a grovelling. At the Eucharist we try with great wonder to grasp the incredible fact that such a God should suffer to make our worship of Him possible.

Inscribed on a plaque in Pleshey retreat house are some words by Evelyn Underhill, which may express something of what we feel: 'Blessed be God that He is God alone and divinely like Himself.'

It is the Church's worship

So when we attend public worship, we come as the Church. We are not merely individuals, we are the body of Christ coming to the one who is our head. We are about the Church's business. This means three things. First, we are the Church adoring, thanking and praising its Lord. We are also the Church of Christ praying for the redemption of all creation. Thirdly, we are a witness to the world for which we pray, a witness that we belong to and serve God.

Despite its divisions, weaknesses and sin, the Church is an impressive thing to belong to. In our little parish or local church we are a fragment of the vast world-wide Church. We may seem small, our congregation may be the usual few whom we see every Sunday, and we may feel we are a rather ineffective group. To make the effort of seeing ourselves as part of Christ's world-wide body can raise us up into loftier spheres of understanding and encourage us to be the Church in a more positive fashion. We are not alone, and the greatness of our Faith can spur us on to enliven the content and witness of our congregation. Great things are happening in the Church all over the world at the present time and not least in our own land. Churches *are* coming to new life and there is a sense of expectation as they increase in prayer, growth, service and witness. Ellerton's words give some expression of the vision of the Church:

The sun that bids us rest is waking
  Our brethren 'neath the western sky,
And hour by hour fresh lips are making
  Thy wondrous doings heard on high.

Our part

Each of us, of course, has a part to play in the total life of the Church and we should not dismiss what we can do as unimportant. It is the sum of the offering of faithful Christians which is the quiet power of the Church's life. What has been already said, therefore, of the quality of our personal prayer is appropriate here also. If we bring an awareness of God's presence and a lively prayer relationship with God to the worship, we shall do our part to bring about the consciousness that 'Surely the Lord is in this place'. If, in addition, we help create an atmosphere of warmth and caring, we shall make a true fellowship of the Spirit. These two things will combine to raise the congregation to true worship.

We each contribute by the way we approach the service and respond to its various parts. It helps if some, at least, arrive early and pray for the strong presence of the Holy Spirit. They can offer to God those taking a particular part—the clergy or ministers, organist and choir, servers, readers, sidespeople. The aim should be for all the congregation to arrive in good time and be praying before the service. If so, there will be a quiet atmosphere before the service begins.

There is, one realises, a difference of opinion about this. Some opt to create an atmosphere of friendliness by chatting to people. Others prefer as near silence as possible to engender an atmosphere conducive to worship. Perhaps this is preferable, with opportunity for sociability afterwards. Of course, if the service is a family service, quietness beforehand is not possible, yet even then, if enough people are at prayer, the effect will be felt. To have some time of silence during the service is important. If this is a regular practice and each week occurs at the same point in the service, people can adjust to it and a strong sense of the presence of God will come. Best of all is when the Holy Spirit so powerfully takes over that the whole congregation is held in unmoving stillness, caught up by God.

We can each do more. We should truly and from the heart pray the prayers of the service and expect the readings of the lessons and the sermon to speak to us. We should sing the hymns, psalms and choruses with understanding. If we are reading a lesson we should understand its meaning, find out how to pronounce the words and speak clearly and slowly. The organist and choir should see themselves as an integral part of the congregation, there to serve in the worship and not to provide a musical concert. As we each so give, we can help the others in church to take their part. If all do this, what an uplifting experience worship can be.

A special responsibility is on the priest or minister leading the service. If it is liturgical, it is incumbent upon the priest to pray the service, not merely to read it. He will then do it unhurriedly and the congregation will be led into worship. A priest or minister will always reveal the quality of his prayer relationship with God by the way he takes the service. There can be a problem when parishes use more than one prayer book because the celebrant has to pay careful attention to each, so as not to slip into the wrong words. Nevertheless, if he is a man of prayer it will be evident.

Almost all denominations have some set form of worship. Even if this form is a simple one as in some Nonconformist churches, people have to adjust to the fact that the service is not designed for their own personal needs. If there is a full liturgy, as in the Anglican Church, people can at first have difficulty, but when the true nature of public worship is recognised, this will not persist. On the contrary, a liturgical form has advantages. Apart from the fact that one is not almost completely dependent upon the contribution of the minister, to share in a liturgy and be carried along by it speaks to something important within us. It is bigger than ourselves. We are encouraged and supported in the knowledge that we are held in worship greater than our own feeble efforts. It is framed by our Mother, the Church, and we can find our security in it. Since it is the quintessence of centuries of worship, it has passed the test of time and has therefore shown that it speaks to the heart of human nature and need. As we share in it regularly it becomes part of ourselves and greatly loved. Free worship, as has been described earlier, does provide a necessary form of worship for one area of our personality, but it entails a constant alertness in order to follow what is going on. Part of us also needs worship with which we are familiar and which we can rest in as it carries us along. It is right that we should worship God in as varied a way as we can, for each form enriches the others.

In the liturgy, also, the Church takes us through the whole range of the Christian year. What a gift the seasons are! Each year we are led into the mysteries and glories of our Faith and therefore can learn to live out the significance of them. So, for example, Advent and Lent are golden opportunities to examine ourselves and prepare for the festivals of Christmas and Easter. We enter for ourselves into the significance of Christmas as Jesus is born in us, and into Easter as we learn to be crucified with Christ by dying to ourself and to sin, and as we are raised into the resurrection life of Christ.

The personal side

So, though our worship is public worship, there is a personal element in it. As we give, so we receive. And this, above all, in the Eucharist, when we receive the Lord Himself. How this expresses the centrality of our Faith! Christ comes to us from His cross and passion through the consecrated elements of His body and blood. He gives Himself to us, bringing His redemption and divine life. We, in turn, receive Him gladly, opening ourselves to Him and giving Him the love of our hearts. So we are made one. God and man are united in love. This great moment can be savoured if time is given to performing the ablutions immediately after the congregation has received. Kneeling in the quietness of our hearts, we can adore and love the Lord whom we have received sacramentally.

Spiritual problems regarding the Eucharist

At this point it might be well to mention matters which cause concern and even shame to quite a few people with regard to the sacrament. One is the temptation not to receive the sacrament when we are in a poor or disturbed spiritual state because we feel that then we are not worthy. This can also be the case when troubled with some sin. Certainly we ought to be in as true a state of repentance as we can, but at times the sin or problem is too much for us and we have not worked through to repentance or a proper grappling with it. In such circumstances some people feel that they are desecrating the sacrament and refrain from receiving. If they truly are wishing to be right with God, however, this would seem to be the wrong attitude. In their weak state they *need* the grace of the sacrament and so they should receive it in an attitude of contrition, gratefully availing themselves of the help Christ will give.

In another quite different situation, there are those who are in emotional suffering which causes a hopelessness and deadness regarding spiritual things. Here it is important that they receive the sacrament regularly, even if it seemingly means nothing to them. Their spirit is still capable of receiving the grace God gives and also the love of God will work within to meet their inner condition.

The third situation is that at such holy moments some people have sexual thoughts which cause them great grief and self-condemnation. This is a common experience and it has not been confined to this century. This is one of the times when the writers of the spiritual life of past times can come to our help. St John of the Cross, a sixteenth-century mystic of Spain, discusses this in Chapter 4 of his work, *The Dark Night of the Soul.* There he says, in effect, that when God touches our love (St John of the Cross calls it the soul) as He does in worship, He touches *all* our love, and this includes our sexual love. Hence sexual thoughts may come to the mind and this can cause shame and deter people from receiving the sacrament, or if they do, it is with self-contempt.

St John of the Cross says that the cleansing comes about as one passes through the dark night of the soul. That is, of course true. But many Christians have not even heard of this dark night and so another way of help must be given. It is suggested that we turn for help to the incarnation of our Lord. The incarnation means that Christ came right into the total sin of man, and by entering into it He broke its power. So, if we have these sexual thoughts, we should receive the sacrament gladly and ask the Lord to enter into this state of sensuality within us and forgive and cleanse it. This, of course, applies to all our sin. Jesus longs to enter into it so that He may deal with it. It is the measure of His love that He does so. Therefore, we should take Him into all our sin, deeply thankful that we have such a God. As Julian of Norwich tells us, sin should not keep us from God. He does not blame us for sinning, she tells us. No, He dies for us and gives Himself to us to cleanse and free us. We can turn this situation into positive action also. Because our sensual love is touched, it can assure us that God is moving within us to raise our soul to love Him. We can, then, take this as such a sign, and respond to Him, allowing ourselves to rise up through the sensual into the spiritual realm of love.

The renewal and the Eucharist

Though the renewal has been a release and given a new freedom of worship under the Holy Spirit, the Spirit has at the same time enhanced the Eucharist. The following are some of the ways in which people have found the sacrament enriched. As He has brought our Lord Jesus Christ more clearly to the centre of our devotion, this has resulted in a new awareness and love for Him in the Eucharist, which centres on His sacrifice for us.

So we find in charismatic worship that the Spirit helps us to enter more fully into the service. So we are led into silent contemplation of the Scriptures after they are read, to allow the Spirit to open them to our hearts. He also leads to freedom at the intercessions and the Peace. This can greatly enrich both. The Intercessions can be more alive and be offered with confidence in Christ, and the Peace becomes a warm and releasing experience. After the Peace, the whole atmosphere of the worship can change in warmth and liveliness. We have come together. The worship rises with this realisation of being one.

This action of the Spirit to make Jesus central in

the worship is seen in what is called the epiclesis, or the prayer of consecration of the bread and wine. In the Alternative Service Book all these prayers ask the Holy Spirit to make the bread and wine the body and blood of our Lord. This liturgical innovation is enhanced by the charismatic experience which makes us spiritually aware of Christ. We expect Him to be involved at the centre of this mystery. One notices that, as a result, some who previously held a 'remembrance' theology have changed to a realisation that our Lord is present and active within the sacrament. The stronger this awareness of Christ becomes, the greater is our faith in the efficacy of the sacrament both in the receiving of Christ's life for growth in grace and in the defeat of sin and Satan.

Finally, a very noticeable effect of the Holy Spirit's action in the Eucharist is that after the receiving of the elements there can come an increased sense of the presence of God. This leads to a spontaneous rise of worship, praise and thanksgiving and with it there may be a ministering of the gifts of the Spirit. Prophecy, tongues and interpretation, visions and singing in tongues come at this point with a facility which can be ascribed only to the strong awareness of Christ among us. It is a time of both uplift and rest in God and brings the service to a consummation of joy under the blessing of God.

14

He is Lord

In Psalm 8 some arresting words describe our relationship with God:

When I consider your heavens,
  the work of your fingers,
the moon and the stars,
  which you have set in place,
what is man that you are mindful of him,
  the son of man that you care for him?
You made him a little lower than the heavenly beings
  and crowned him with glory and honour
(vv. 3–5, NIV).

God's majesty is such that humanity seems almost to be barely worthy of His attention. Yet our destiny is to share His majesty. So great is God and our comprehension so small that we have to make Him small. To many, perhaps unconsciously, He is seen as a big man. It is through worship and wonder that we glimpse more, though the nearer we get the less we can express.

We should be grateful for the Book of Revelation where, more than anywhere else in the Bible, the reality of adoration and worship of God is presented to us. While the essence of the unutterable glory of God cannot be expressed in words, passages in that book give a vivid indication of it. They excite our hearts and create a longing to share it.

In one passage we read, 'Then I looked, and I heard around the throne and the living creatures and the elders the voice of many angels, numbering myriads of myriads and thousands of thousands, saying with a loud voice, "Worthy is the Lamb who was slain, to receive power and wealth and wisdom and might and honor and glory and blessing!" And I heard every creature in heaven and on earth and in the sea, and all therein, saying, "To him who sits upon the throne and to the Lamb be blessing and honor and glory and might for ever and ever!"' (5.11–13).

This is a graphic picture of all creation, the angel hierarchy, humanity and everything that has being, exulting in God. Much of creation cannot adore consciously, but it does so by the very fact of its being. God has made it, and so it glorifies Him. For the same reason, all of us are part of this universal adoration. We come to the height of our existence when we realise this and offer our part in the worship consciously and gladly.

The transfiguration of Christ provides another glimmer of light as we seek to share something of the glory of God. In the book of Revelation we have the proclaiming of the wonder of God in creation. On the mountain we cross the divide of death. Our Lord, Moses and Elijah are in a glory, the sight of which terrifies Peter, James and John.

Maybe it is all as we would expect. Moses and Elijah, coming from the realms of glory, would naturally appear glorious. Jesus, God in human form, does not surprise us. But the glory so revealed in Jesus at that moment was normally hidden. Usually it expressed itself in ways humanity could appreciate —words such as no other man spoke, compassion never seen to such an extent in humanity, power to heal and control nature, a majestic personality—but the essential glory was hidden.

Seeing the glory, the disciples were filled with fear. So that they could be in a condition to hear God's voice, a cloud had to hide the glory that frightened them. It was not until Jesus was again seen in His normal appearance that they could be at ease with Him.

So it seems that those who belong to Christ in this world have His glory within though, as with their Lord, it is seen indirectly in the way it has changed their lives. Perhaps the losing of the body after the divide of death will reveal the hidden glory, the glory in us through Christ's redemption. This is another aspect of the book of Revelation's insistence on God's glory in all creation. Perhaps, too, as with the disciples, this is the only way we, in our present state, can bear the glory in each other. When Christ is hidden in humanity His glory is not too much for us. Nor are our fellow human beings who are in Christ too much for us.

Arthur Blessit in his book *Turned on to Jesus* (Word Books, 1972) records how he and a friend had a vision of Christ which resulted in both of them glowing with light. When their wives saw them, they were terrified and would have nothing to do with them. Arthur's wife screamed and ran from him, and neither wife could bear to be with her husband. Later, Arthur's wife was able to sit near to him. 'The glow is gone,' she said, 'I'm not afraid to be close to you any more' (pp. 91–5). So, while God's glory surrounds and is within us, it seems best for us that we see little of it. But it is there and it should hearten us to know that we are so much enfolded in His glory.

We each walk our own way in this spiritual pilgrimage into glory as the Holy Spirit awakens in our heart the desire for God Himself. When He does, prayer means more than praying for ourselves and our needs. We begin fixing our desire upon God Himself. Every Christian should ask the Spirit for this desire. It is God who gives it us—and in this way raises us from earth to heaven, for Christ came 'that he might bring us to God' (1 Pet. 3.18). The hope is that this book will encourage this adventure by prayer and worship into the life of God. When our whole self is in God, nothing in our life fails to benefit. Just one among many blessings which is of particular importance today is the confidence God gives. In a world which is negative, bewildered and fearful, prayer and worship which are a true meeting with God bring us the realisation that God is our eternal rock in whom we can have full confidence. So our lives will be positive and full of hope. They will have direction and a purpose, and we will not depend upon this world. Such a confidence is infectious. So with Paul we can praise 'the blessed and only Sovereign, the King of kings and Lord of lords, who alone had immortality and dwells in unapproachable light, whom no man has ever seen or can see. To him be honor and eternal dominion. Amen' (1 Tim. 6.15–16).

Appendix

Further reading

For a description of contemplative prayer, *The Inner Eye of Love: Mysticism and Religion* by William Johnston (London, Collins, 1978 and Fount paperback edition) is recommended. It is written in a non-technical style and so the ideas are not difficult to understand.

Contemplative writings

The following is a very selective list of writings of a contemplative nature. These and many others should be available in libraries, and most are in print at reasonable prices.

The Cloud of Unknowing
Written by a fourteenth-century Englishman, it is the best guide we have to contemplative prayer. A delightful book. Editions available include a modern translation by Halcyon C. Backhouse (Hodder & Stoughton, London, 1985).

Julian of Norwich, *Revelations of Divine Love* (Harmondsworth, Penguin, 1973)

Also a fourteenth-century writer, but a woman. It is a book one constantly returns to. *Enfolded in Love* (Norwich, Julian Shrine, 1980) consists of daily readings and is also a treasury of spiritual nourishment. There is a fascinating homeliness about this mystic.

Teresa of Avila, *The Way of Perfection* (Sheed & Ward, London, 1982) and *The Life of the Holy Mother Teresa of Jesus* (Sheed & Ward, London, 1979) are two books by a sixteenth-century Spanish contemplative, and were written for her nuns. They are full of sound teaching and wit and are very much down to earth.

Jean Pierre de Caussade, *Self Abandonment to Divine Providence*

A fine work by a French Jesuit. The main idea is that we find God in the present moment: Kitty Muggeridge's translation (Fount, London, 1981) is entitled *The Sacrament of the Present Moment.*

Brother Lawrence, *The Practice of the Presence of God* (trans. D. Attwater, Burns & Oates, London, 1977; trans. E. M. Blaiklock, Hodder & Stoughton, London, 1981)

A small but delightful book. It is a collection of conversations and a few letters by a peasant who became a monk and a great man of prayer.

Jean-Nicolas Grou, *Marks of True Devotion* (Burns & Oates, London, 1963) and *Manual for Interior Souls* (Orchard Series, Burns & Oates, London, 1948)

By a Frenchman who lived in the eighteenth century. Good teaching, and useful for daily devotional reading.

Abbé de Tourville, *Letters of Direction: Thoughts on the Spiritual Life from the Letters of the Abbé* (Mowbray, Oxford, 1982)

Excellent daily reading with positive teaching on the Christian life and eminently sensible.

Thérèse of Lisieux, *The Story of a Soul* (Anthony Clarke, Wheathampstead, 1973)

The autobiography and spiritual growth of a nineteenth-century French nun. She died at 24, yet gave so much.

The Eastern Church

The Way of a Pilgrim (trans. R. M. French, SPCK, London, 1930)

A delightful account of the Jesus Prayer.

Some paperbacks by present-day members of the Orthodox Churches:

Metropolitan Anthony Bloom, *Living Prayer* (Darton, Longman & Todd, London, 1966) and *School for Prayer* (Darton, Longman & Todd, London, 1970)

Two general books on prayer.

Archimandrite Sophrony, *His Life is Mine* (Mowbray, Oxford, 1978)

Prayer from an Eastern monk's experience. Part 2 is devoted to the Jesus Prayer in some depth.

Catherine de Hueck Doherty, *Poustinia* (Fount, London, 1977)

Eastern spirituality lived out in a Western setting.

Other books

Baron Friedrich von Hugel, *The Life of Prayer* (J. M. Dent, London, 1927)

By a master of the spiritual life.

Henri Nouwen, *The Genesee Diary: a Report from a Trappist Monastery* (Doubleday, New York, 1976)
This is his diary of seven months' struggle with Jesus Christ. His other books are also illuminating, for example *With Open Hands* (Ave Maria, USA, 1975). There may be an English paperback available now.

Thomas Merton, *Contemplative Prayer* (Darton, Longman & Todd, London, 1973)
All his books are helpful.

Spiritual Autobiography of Charles de Foucauld edited by Jean-Francois Six (Anthony Clarke Books, Wheathampstead & Dimension Books, New Jersey, 1964) (Joint publication).
The writings of a man who left Western society for the desert, to live a life of poverty and contemplation. The Little Brothers and Sisters have sprung from him. Their founder, René Voillaume, has written of their way of life in the centre of the modern world; his books include *Seeds of the Desert: Like Jesus of Nazareth* (Anthony Clarke Books, Wheathampstead, 1982) and *The Need for Contemplation* (Darton, Longman & Todd, London, 1972)

Fynn, *Mister God this is Anna* (Collins, London, 1974 and Fount paperback edition)
A little girl who was a natural mystic. Fascinating and enchanting.

Charles Williams, novels.
In an imaginative way they take us into the realm of the unseen.

Other Marshall Pickering Paperbacks

THROUGH DAVID'S PSALMS

Derek Prince

Derek Prince, internationally known Bible teacher and scholar, draws on his understanding of the Hebrew language and culture, and a comprehensive knowledge of Scripture, to present 101 meditations from the Psalms.
Each of these practical and enriching meditations is based on a specific passage and concludes with a faith response. They can be used either for personal meditation or for family devotions. They are intended for all those who want their lives enriched or who seek comfort and encouragement from the Scriptures.

LOVING GOD

Charles Colson

Loving God is the very purpose of the believer's life, the vocation for which he is made. However loving God is not easy and most people have given little real thought to what the greatest commandment really means.
Many books have been written on the individual subjects of repentence, Bible study, prayer, outreach, evangelism, holiness and other elements of the Christian life. In **Loving God**, Charles Colson draws all these elements together to look at the entire process of growing up as a Christian.
Combining vivid illustrations with straightforward exposition he shows how to live out the Christian faith in our daily lives. **Loving God** provides a real challenge to deeper commitment and points the way towards greater maturity.

HOW TO MANAGE PRESSURE
Before Pressure Manages You

Tim LaHaye

Pressure is unavoidable. Everyone faces pressure in some area of their life. Even as you read this, you may be aware of pressures in your life that cause worry and tension and hinder your sense of well being.

The good news of this book is that there is a way to handle pressure so that it can become a creative rather than destructive force.

Tim LaHaye offers insights that will enable you to relieve stress and to live a more satisfying life amidst those everyday pressures.

LOVE LIFE FOR EVERY MARRIED COUPLE

Dr E. Wheat

Dr Wheat, a physician and therapist, has helped thousands of troubled couples improve their love lives and build happier marriages with his unique counselling methods. In **Love Life for Every Married Couple**, Dr Wheat explores marital conflict in a straightforward manner, focusing on the reasons why couples experience frustration and unhappiness in their love lives.

"Dr Wheat has revealed, again, his unique talent for identifying the critical issues in family living, and then offering wise counsel and loving support to those who hurt . . . I recommend Love Life to those who want a better marriage."
Dr James Dobson

If you wish to receive *regular information* about *new books*, please send your name and address to:

London Bible Warehouse
PO Box 123
Basingstoke
Hants RG23 7NL

Name ______________________________

Address ____________________________

____

____

____

I am especially interested in:

- ☐ Biographies
- ☐ Fiction
- ☐ Christian living
- ☐ Issue related books
- ☐ Academic books
- ☐ Bible study aids
- ☐ Children's books
- ☐ Music
- ☐ Other subjects

P.S. If you have ideas for new Christian Books or other products, please write to us too!